# SAVING THE APPEARANCES

# Saving the Appearances

*A Study in Idolatry*

*by*

OWEN BARFIELD

A Harvest/HBJ Book
Harcourt Brace Jovanovich
New York and London

*Library of Congress Catalog Card Number: 65-23538*
*Printed in the United States of America*

GHIJ

To
MY BROTHER

# FOREWORD

My warm thanks are due to several of my friends for the interest they have taken in this book; particularly to my brother Dr. R. H. Barfield (to whom it is dedicated), Mr. T. A. Barfield, Mr. and Mrs. Charles Davy, Sir George Rostrevor Hamilton and Professor C. S. Lewis, all of whom have favoured me with thoughtful comments and practical suggestions, which I have used freely; above all to Dr. A. P. Shepherd for wise aid and counsel with my first draft of the earlier chapters on the table between us.

# CONTENTS

# Contents

# INTRODUCTION

There may be times when what is most needed is, not so much a new discovery or a new idea as a different 'slant'; I mean a comparatively slight readjustment in our *way* of looking at the things and ideas on which attention is already fixed.

Draw a rectangular glass box in perspective—not too precise perspective (for the receding lines must be kept parallel, instead of converging)—and look at it. It has a front and a back, a top and a bottom. But slide your hand across it in the required direction and look again: you may find that what you thought was the inside of the top has become its outside, while the outside of the front wall has changed to the inside of the back wall, and vice versa. The visual readjustment was slight, but the effect on the drawing has been far from slight, for the box has not only turned inside out but is also lying at quite a different angle.

The book which follows has been written in the belief that it might be possible to slide a sort of hand across a good many of the things and ideas upon which the attention of western humanity has been concentrated for the last two or three hundred years, and upon which the attention of the East is rapidly becoming fixed in the same way. The helping 'hand' which it has been sought to apply in this way is, simply, a *sustained* acceptance by the reader of the relation assumed by physical science to subsist between human consciousness on the one hand and, on the other, the familiar world of which that consciousness is aware.

# Introduction

Physical science has for a long time stressed the enormous difference between what it investigates as the actual structure of the universe, including the earth, and the phenomena, or appearances, which are presented by that structure to normal human consciousness. In tune with this, most philosophy—at all events since Kant—has heavily emphasized the participation of man's own mind in the creation, or evocation, of these phenomena. The first three short chapters are largely devoted to reminding the reader of that difference and that participation.

About this conception of the relation between man and nature, which is wholly undisputed outside academic philosophy and largely undisputed within it, two things are noticeable; though they do not appear as yet to have been very widely noticed. One is an omission and the other an assumption.

In the first place, undisputed though it remains, it is (if we except a certain school of genetic psychology, now very much out of fashion) always left out of account in our approach to any subject outside the sphere of physics—such subjects, for example, as the history of the earth, the history of language, the history of thought. In the second place, it is invariably assumed that, whatever the truth may be about the psychological nexus between man and nature, it is an unchanging one and is the same now as it was when men first appeared on earth.

In this book it is suggested that the assumption arose in the first place through clearly traceable historical causes; that the evidence is in favour of regarding it as illusory; and that its persistence in spite of that evidence is largely due to the omission.

As to the omission: having established the gulf which yawns between the atomic physical structure of nature and the appearances of the familiar world, it is of course possible, it is certainly usual—if we are physicists, to continue undisturbed with our investigations of the unappearing atomic structure, and, if we are philosophers, to leave it at that, being content with the metaphysical curiosity we have produced. It is usual; but it is not really necessary to do so. We could, if we chose, take it seriously; we could keep the gulf steadily in sight, instead of instantly forgetting all about it again, and see what effect that has on our knowledge of other things, such as the evolution of nature and of man himself. Nor does this seem an unreasonable undertaking, since these are both matters, and the relation between them is a matter, to which the participation mentioned four paragraphs back must be at least relevant.

The greater part of this book consists, in fact, of a rudimentary attempt to remedy the omission. But this involves, as already indicated, challenging the assumption; and a good deal of attention has been devoted to that aspect also. The result—and really the substance of the book—is a sort of outline sketch, with one or two parts completed in greater detail, for a history of human consciousness; particularly the consciousness of western humanity during the last three thousand years or so.

Finally, the consequences which flow from abandoning the assumption are found to be very far-reaching; and the last three chapters are concerned, theologically, with the bearing of 'participation'—viewed now as an historical process—upon the origin, the predicament, and the destiny of man.

# I

## THE RAINBOW

Look at a rainbow. While it lasts, it is, or appears to be, a great arc of many colours occupying a position out there in space. It touches the horizon between that chimney and that tree; a line drawn from the sun behind you and passing through your head would pierce the centre of the circle of which it is part. And now, before it fades, recollect all you have ever been told about the rainbow and its causes, and ask yourself the question *Is it really there?*

You know, from memory, that if there were a hillside three or four miles nearer than the present horizon, the rainbow would come to earth in front of and not behind it; that, if you walked to the place where the rainbow ends, or seems to end, it would certainly not be 'there'. In a word, reflection will assure you that the rainbow is the outcome of the sun, the raindrops and your own vision.

When I ask of an intangible appearance or representation, Is it really there? I usually mean, Is it there independently of my vision? Would it still be there, for instance, if I shut my eyes—if I moved towards or away from it. If this is what you also mean by 'really there', you will be tempted to add that the raindrops and the sun are really there, but the rainbow is not.

Does it follow that, as soon as anybody sees a rainbow, there 'is' one, or, in other words, that there is no difference between an hallucination or a madman's dream of a rainbow (perhaps on a clear day) and an actual rainbow? Certainly not. You were not the only one to see that rainbow. You had a friend with you. (I forbear asking if you both saw 'the same' rainbow, because this is a book about history rather than metaphysics, and these introductory chapters are merely intended to clear away certain misconceptions.) Moreover, through the medium of language, you are well aware that thousands of others have seen rainbows in showery weather; but you have never heard of any sane person claiming to have seen one on a sunless or a cloudless day. Therefore, if a man tells you he sees a rainbow on a cloudless day, then, even if you are convinced that he means what he says, and is not simply lying, you will confidently affirm that the rainbow he sees is 'not there'.

In short, as far as being really there or not is concerned, the practical difference between a dream or hallucination of a rainbow and an actual rainbow is that, although each is a representation or appearance (that is, something which I perceive to be there), the second is a *shared* or collective representation.

Now look at a tree. It is very different from a rainbow. If you approach it, it will still be 'there'. Moreover, in this case, you can do more than look at it. You can hear the noise its leaves make in the wind. You can perhaps smell it. You can certainly touch it. Your senses combine to assure you that it is composed of what is called solid matter. Accord to the tree the same treatment that you accorded to the rainbow. Recollect all you have been told about matter and its ultimate structure and ask yourself if the tree is 'really there'. I am far from affirming dogmatically that the atoms, electrons, nuclei, etc., of which wood, and all matter, is said to be composed, are particular and identifiable objects like drops of rain. But if the 'particles' (as I will here call them for convenience) *are* there, and are all that is there, then, since the 'particles' are no more like the thing I call a tree than the raindrops are like the thing I call a rainbow, it follows, I think, that—just as a rainbow is the outcome of the raindrops and my vision—so, a tree is the outcome of the particles and my vision and my other sense-perceptions. Whatever the particles themselves may be thought to be, the tree, as such, is a representation. And the difference, for me, between a tree and a complete hallucination of a tree is the same as the difference between a rainbow and an hallucination of a rainbow. In other words, a tree which is 'really there' is a collective representation. The fact that a dream tree differs in kind from a real tree, and that it is just silly to try and mix them up, is indeed rather literally a matter of 'common sense'.

This background of particles is of course presumed in the case of raindrops themselves, no less than in that of trees. The relation, *raindrops: rainbow*, is a picture or analogy, not an instance, of the relation, *particles: representation*.

Or again, if anyone likes to press the argument still further and maintain that what is true of the drops must also be true of the particles themselves, and that there is 'no such thing as an extra-mental reality', I shall not quarrel with him, but I shall leave him severely alone; because, as I say, this is not a book about metaphysics, and I have no desire to demonstrate that trees or rainbows—or particles—are not 'really there'—a proposition which perhaps has not much meaning. This book is not being written because the author desires to put forward a theory of perception, but because it seems to him that certain wide consequences flowing from the hastily expanded sciences of the nineteenth and twentieth centuries, and in particular their physics, have not been sufficiently considered in building up the general twentieth-century picture of the nature of the universe and of the history of the earth and man.

A better term than 'particles' would possibly be 'the unrepresented', since anything particular which amounts to a representation will always attract further physical analysis. Moreover, the atoms, protons and electrons of modern physics are now perhaps more generally regarded, not as particles, but as notional models or symbols of an unknown supersensible or subsensible base. All I seek to establish in these opening paragraphs is, that, whatever may be thought about the 'unrepresented' background of our perceptions, the *familiar* world which we see and know around us—the blue sky with white clouds in it, the noise of a waterfall or a motor-bus, the shapes of flowers and their scent, the gesture and utterance of animals and the faces of our friends —the world too, which (apart from the special inquiry of physics) experts of all kinds methodically investigate—is a system of collective representations. The time comes when one must either accept this as the truth about the world or reject the theories of physics as an elaborate delusion. We cannot have it both ways.

## II

## COLLECTIVE REPRESENTATIONS

A representation is something I perceive to be there. By premising that the everyday world is a system of collective representations, it may be thought that we blur the distinction between the fancied and the actual or, following the everyday use of language, between the apparently there and the really there. But this is not so. It only seems to be so because of the very great emphasis which—especially in the last three or four hundred years—the Western Mind has come to lay on the ingredient of spatial depth in the total complex of its perception. I shall return to this later.

As to what is meant by 'collective'—any discrepancy between my representations and those of my fellow men raises a presumption of unreality and calls for explanation. If, however, the explanation is satisfactory; if, for instance, it turns out that the discrepancy was due, not to my hallucination, but to their myopia or their dullness, it is likely to be accepted; and then my representation may itself end by becoming collective.

It is, however, not necessary to maintain that collectivity is the *only* test for distinguishing between a representation and a collective representation (though, to creatures for whom insanity is round the corner, it is often likely to be the crucial one).

I am hit violently on the head and, in the same moment, perceive a bright light to be there. Later on I reflect that the light was 'not really there'. Even if I had lived all my life on a desert island where there was no-one to compare notes with, I might do as much. No doubt I should learn by experience to distinguish the first kind of light from the more practicable light of day or the thunderbolt, and should soon give up hitting myself on the head at sunset when I needed light to go on working by. In both cases I perceive light, but the various criteria of difference between them—duration, for instance, and a sharp physical pain, which the one involves and the other does not, are not difficult to apprehend.

What is required, is not to go on stressing the resemblance between collective representations and private representations, but to remember, when we leave the world of everyday for the discipline of any strict inquiry, that, *if* the particles, or the unrepresented, are in fact all that is *independently* there, then the world we all accept as real is in fact a system of collective representations.

Perception takes place by means of sense-organs, though the ingredient in it of sensation, experienced as such, varies greatly as between the different senses. In touch I suppose we come nearest to sensation without perception; in sight to perception without sensation. But the two most important things to remember about perception are these: *first*, that we must not confuse the percept with its cause. I do not hear undulating molecules of air; the name of what I hear is *sound*. I do not touch a moving system of waves or of atoms and electrons with relatively vast empty spaces between them; the name of what I touch is *matter*. *Second*, I do not perceive any *thing* with my sense-organs alone, but with a great part of my whole human being. Thus, I may say, loosely, that I 'hear a thrush singing'. But in strict truth all that I ever merely 'hear'—all that I ever hear simply by virtue of having ears—is *sound*. When I 'hear a thrush singing', I am hearing, not with my ears alone, but with all sorts of other things like mental habits, memory, imagination, feeling and (to the extent at least that the act of attention involves it) will. Of a man who merely heard in the first

20

sense, it could meaningfully be said that 'having ears' (i.e. not being deaf) 'he heard not'.

I do not think either of these two maxims depends on any particular theory of the nature of perception. They are true for any theory of perception I ever heard of—with the possible exception of Bishop Berkeley's.[1] They are true, whether we accept the Aristotelian and medieval conception of form and matter, or the Kantian doctrine of the forms of perception, or the theory of specific sense-energy, or the 'primary imagination' of Coleridge, or the phenomenology that underlies Existentialism, or some wholly unphilosophical system of physiology and psychology. On almost any received theory of perception the familiar world—that is, the world which is apprehended, not through instruments and inference, but simply—is for the most part dependent upon the percipient.

[1] Cf. p. 38.

# III

## FIGURATION AND THINKING

In the conversion of raindrops into a rainbow, or (if you prefer it) the production of a rainbow out of them, the *eye* plays a no less indispensable part than the sunlight—or than the drops themselves. In the same way, for the conversion of the unrepresented into a representation, at least one sentient organism is as much a *sine qua non* as the unrepresented itself; and for the conversion of the unrepresented into representations even remotely resembling our everyday world, at least one nervous system organized about a spinal cord culminating in a brain, is equally indispensable. The rainbow analogy does not imply, nor is it intended to suggest, that the solid globe is as insubstantial as a rainbow. The solid globe is solid. The rainbow is not. Only it is important to know what we mean by solidity. More than that, it is necessary to remember what we meant by solidity in one context, when we go on to use the word or think the thing in another.

It is easy to appreciate that there is no such thing as an unseen rainbow. It is not so easy to grasp that there is no such thing as an unheard noise. Or rather it is easy to grasp, but difficult to keep hold of. And this is still more the case, when we come to the sense of touch. Obvious as it may be to reflection that a system of waves or quanta or discrete particles is no more like solid matter than waves of air are like sound, or raindrops like a rainbow, it is not particularly easy to grasp, and it is almost impossible to keep in mind,

22

that there is no such thing as unfelt solidity.[1] It is much more convenient, when we are listening for example to the geologist, to forget what we learnt about matter from the chemist and the physicist. But it really will not do. We cannot go on for ever having it both ways.

It may be expedient at this point to examine a little further the collective representations and our thinking about them. And it is clearly of little use to begin by asking what they are; since they are everything that is obvious. They are, for instance, the desk I am writing at, the noise of a door being opened downstairs, a Union Jack, an altar in a Church, the smell of coffee, a totem pole, the view from Malvern Hills, and the bit of brain-tissue that is being dissected before a group of students in a hospital laboratory. Some of them we can manipulate, as the lecturer is doing, and as I do when I move the desk. Some of them we cannot. What is important here is that there are, broadly speaking, three different things that we can do with all of them; or, alternatively, they are related to the mind in three different ways.

First, we can simply contemplate or experience them—as when I simply look at the view, or encounter the smell. The whole impression appears then to be given to me in the representation itself. For I am not, or I am not very often, aware of smelling an unidentified smell and then thinking, 'That is coffee!' It appears to me, and appears instantly, that I smell coffee—though, in fact, I can no more merely *smell* 'coffee' than I can merely *hear* 'a thrush singing'. This immediate impression or experience of a familiar world has already been mentioned in Chapter II. It is important to be clear about it. It is plainly the result of an activity of some sort in me, however little I may recollect any such activity.

---

[1] 'The thermometer is below freezing point, the pipe is cracked, and no water comes out of the tap. I know nothing about physics or chemistry; but surely I can say that there is solid ice in the pipe!' Certainly you can; and if there was salt in the water, you can say that there is solid, *white* ice in the pipe. I am only pointing out that the solidity you are talking about involves your fancied touch, just as the whiteness involves your fancied glance. Only it is harder to remember.

# Figuration and Thinking

When a lady complained to Whistler that she did not see the world he painted, he is said to have replied: 'No, ma'am, but don't you wish you could?' Both Whistler and the lady were really referring to that activity—which in Whistler's case was intenser than the lady's. Ought it to be called a 'mental' activity? Whatever it ought to be called, it really is the percipient's own contribution to the representation. It is all *that* in the representation which is not sensation. For, as the organs of sense are required to convert the unrepresented ('particles') into sensations for us, so *something* is required in us to convert sensations into 'things'. It is this something that I mean. And it will avoid confusion if I purposely choose an unfamiliar and little-used word and call it, at the risk of infelicity, *figuration*.

Let me repeat it. On the assumption that the world whose existence is independent of our sensation and perception consists solely of 'particles', two operations are necessary (and whether they are successive or simultaneous is of no consequence), in order to produce the familiar world we know. First, the sense-organs must be related to the particles in such a way as to give rise to sensations; and secondly, those mere sensations must be combined and constructed by the percipient mind into the recognizable and nameable objects we call 'things'. It is this work of construction which will here be called *figuration*.

Now whether or no figuration is a mental activity, that is, a kind of thinking, it is clearly not, or it is not *characteristically*, a thinking *about*. The second thing, therefore, that we can do with the representations is to think about them. Here, as before, we remain unconscious of the intimate relation which they in fact have, as representations, with our own organisms and minds. Or rather, more unconscious than before. For now our very attitude is, to treat them as independent of ourselves; to accept their 'outness' as self-evidently given; and to speculate about or to investigate their relations *with each other*. One could perhaps name this process 'theorizing' or 'theoretical thinking', since it is exactly what is done in most places where science is pursued, whether it be botany, medicine, metallurgy, zoology or any other. But I do not think the term is wide enough. The kind of thing I mean covers other studies as well—a good deal of history, for instance. Nor need it be systematic. There are very few children who do not do a little of it. Moreover, if a common word is chosen, there is the same danger of confusion arising from its occasional use with a less precise intention. Therefore, at the like hazard as before, I propose to call this particular kind of thinking *alpha-thinking*.

Thirdly, we can think about the *nature* of collective representations as such, and therefore about their relation to our own minds. We can think about perceiving and we can think about thinking. We can do, in fact, the kind of thinking which I am trying to do at the moment, and which you will be doing if you think I am right and also if you think I am wrong. This is part of the province of one or two sciences such as physiology and psychology, and of course it is also part of the province of philosophy. It has been called reflection or reflective thinking. But for the same reasons as before, I shall reject the simpler and more elegant term and call it *beta-thinking*.

It should be particularly noted that the distinction here made between alpha-thinking and beta-thinking is not one between two different *kinds* of thinking, such as for instance that which is sometimes made between analytical thinking on the one hand and synthetic or imaginative thinking on the other. It is purely a distinction of subject-matters.

The three operations—*figuration*, *alpha-thinking* and *beta-thinking*—are clearly distinguishable from one another; but that is not to say that they are divided by impassable barriers at the points where they mutually approach. Indeed the reverse is true. Moreover they may affect each other by reciprocal influence. In the history of the theory of colour, for instance, colour began by being regarded as a primary quality of the coloured object and was later transferred to the status of a 'secondary' quality dependent on the beholder. Here we can detect the interaction of alpha-thinking and beta-thinking; and again in the whole influence which experimental science has exerted on philosophy in the last two or three hundred years. This book, on the other hand, will be more concerned with the interaction between figuration and alpha-thinking.

That the former of these affects, and largely determines, the latter hardly needs saying; since the primary product of figuration is the actual subject-matter of most alpha-thinking. That the converse may sometimes also be true, and further, that the borderline between the one and the other is sometimes quite impossible to determine—this is less obvious. Yet a little serious reflection (that is, a little beta-thinking) makes it apparent enough.

Recall for a moment the familiar jingle from *Sylvie and Bruno*, with its persistent refrain of 'he thought he saw' followed by 'he found it was':

> He thought he saw a Banker's Clerk
>    Descending from the bus,
> He looked again, and found it was
>    A hippopotamus.
>
> > etc., etc.

This is of course only a very improbable instance of an experience which, in itself, is quite common, especially with those among our representations (and they form the overwhelming majority) which reach us through the sense of sight alone. When we mistake one representation, that is to say one thing, for another, so that there is a transition from an 'I thought I saw' to an 'I found it was', it is often very difficult indeed to say whether there is first a figuration (based, let us say, on incomplete sensation) and then another and different figuration, producing a different representation; or whether there is one and the same representation, veiled from us at first by some incorrect alpha-thinking, which is subsequently discarded as inapplicable. In the particular case of a puzzled man trying to descry an object spotted far off at sea, it feels more like the latter. Often it feels much more like the former. We have made the mistake before we are aware of having done any thinking at all.

Anyone who wishes to investigate this further should attend carefully to the sort of mistakes we are apt to make on awaking abruptly from deep sleep in a darkened room; especially if it happens to be a strange room. Either way we must conclude that figuration, whether or no it is a kind of thinking, is something which easily and imperceptibly passes over into thinking, and into which thinking easily and imperceptibly passes over. For in both cases there was a representation; otherwise I should not have been deceived. And if the first representation was the result of incorrect thinking, then thinking can do something very much like what figuration does. Alternatively, if it was the result of figuration alone, then the very fact that figuration can 'make a mistake' suggests that it has a good deal in common with thinking.

# IV

# PARTICIPATION

In the last few decades this whole question of the figurative make-up of collective representations and the theoretical confusion between what I have called figuration and what I have called alpha-thinking has been implicitly raised by certain anthropologists. Putting it in a nutshell, they have suggested, by the whole manner of their approach to the workings of the 'primitive' mind, the question: Can there be such a thing as, '*They* thought *they* saw?'

Of course, two people can make the same momentary mistake about the identity of an imperfectly seen object. But, as we saw in Chapter II, the generally accepted criterion of the difference between 'I thought I saw' and 'I found it was' is, that the former is a private, the latter a collective representation. How, then, if the 'they' are a whole tribe or population? If the 'mistake' is not a momentary but a permanent one? If it is passed down for centuries from generation to generation? If, in fact, it is *never* followed by a 'they found it was'? The difficulty is, that then the 'mistake' is itself a collective representation. And yet for ourselves, as we saw, it is precisely the collectivity of our representations which is the accepted test of their reality. It is this which convinces us that they are *not* mistakes or hallucinations. Why not then also for them—the primitive tribe? But this is to go too fast.

The earlier anthropologists assumed as a matter of course that the primitive peoples who still survive in various parts of the earth perceive and think in the same *way* as we do—but that they think incorrectly. The assumption which underlies their whole approach to the subject is effectively epitomized in two sentences from Tylor's *Primitive Culture*, first published in 1871:

It was no spontaneous fancy but the reasonable inference that effects are due to causes, which led the rude men of olden days to people with such ethereal phantoms their own houses and haunts and the vast earth and sky beyond. Spirits are personified causes.

This theory of an 'inferring' followed by a 'peopling', which is usually called 'animism', but which Durkheim prefers to call 'naturism', is moreover, according to Lévy-Bruhl, especially typical of the English school of anthropology, and he attributes this, rightly or wrongly, to the influence of Herbert Spencer, who assumed so readily that all things evolve from simple to complex. Be that as it may, the theory is attacked by the twentieth-century anthropologists to whom I have referred. They deny the 'inferring' and question the 'peopling'. Lévy-Bruhl himself, for instance, insists, in the light of the evidence, that to ask how the primitive mind would 'explain' this or that natural phenomenon is a wrongly formulated question. The explanation is implied in the collective representations themselves. When we find a primitive mind incapable of grasping what is to us the self-evident law of contradiction, it is absurd to imagine such a mind thinking in terms of cause and effect, and of inference from the one to the other. Rather we are in contact with a different kind of thinking and a different kind of perceiving altogether. Lévy-Bruhl describes this 'prelogical mentality', which he says is:

essentially synthetic. By this I mean that the syntheses which compose it do not imply previous analyses of which the result has been registered in definite concepts, as is the case with those in which logical thought operates.

In other words, the connecting links of the representations are given, as a rule, in the representations themselves.

This is also found to be a more satisfactory and convincing approach to the phenomenon of totemism, which involves the most inexplicable and, to us, nonsensical identifications and distinctions. To make no class-distinction between the sun and a white cockatoo, but to feel instantly and sharply a world of difference between both of these natural phenomena and a black cockatoo is, it is felt, a state of mind at which it would be difficult to arrive by inference. The elements which the totem-conscious mind selects out of the whole representation for *attention*, are often very very different from those which we select. Often, for instance, it is not much interested in the distinction between animate and inanimate (including artificial) objects.

Almost everything that we see therein (i.e. in a being or object or natural phenomenon) escapes their attention or is a matter of indifference to them. On the other hand they see many things of which we are unconscious.

This leads Lévy-Bruhl to the conclusion that 'Primitives see with eyes like ours, but they do not perceive with the same minds'. And he adds:

It is not correct to maintain, as is frequently done, that primitives associate occult powers, magic properties, a kind of soul or vital principle with all the objects which affect their senses or strike the imagination, and that their perceptions are surcharged with animistic beliefs. It is not a question of *association*. The mystic properties with which things are imbued form an integral part of the idea to the primitive who views it as a synthetic whole. It is at a later stage of social evolution that what we call a natural phenomenon tends to become the sole content of perception to the exclusion of other elements which then assume the aspect of beliefs, and finally appear superstitions. But as long as this 'dissociation' does not take place, perception remains an undifferentiated whole.

It may be questioned whether the epithet 'mystic', as it is used here, and in the expression 'participation mystique' which is especially associated with the name of Lévy-Bruhl, adds effectively to his meaning. Elsewhere he has defined the precise significance which he intends by it, and I shall revert to this shortly. What is important is the concept of participation. The principal reason which Lévy-Bruhl, Durkheim and others assign for the fact that primitives 'do not perceive with the same minds' as ours, is, that in the act of perception, they are not detached, as we are, from the representations. For us the only connection *of which we are conscious* is the external one through the senses. Not so for them. Thus, for Lévy-Bruhl:

> The collective representations and interconnections which constitute such a (primitive) mentality are governed by the law of participation and in so far they take but little account of the law of contradiction.

He speaks of 'a veritable symbiosis . . . between the totemic group and its totem' and tells us that, if we seek to penetrate their mental processes, 'We must understand "the same" by virtue, not of the law of identity, but of the law of participation'.

Durkheim seeks to carry much further the bearing of anthropological inquiry on the origin and evolution of abstract thought. He affirms, for instance, that the identification of persons and individual phenomena with totems violates the principle of contradiction only as predication[1] does in our own thinking. The root or predecessor of predication is to be found in 'the use of totemic emblems by clans to express and communicate collective representations'.

---

[1] *Predication* may be unconventionally, but not really inaccurately, defined as, 'Whatever is done by the word *is* in such a sentence as: *a horse is an animal*; *the earth is a planet*'. See also p. 99.

# Participation

We shall see that this same expression and communication are to-day the function of *language*. 'Participation' begins by being an activity, and essentially a communal or social activity. It takes place in rites and initiation ceremonies resulting in

> collective mental states of extreme emotional intensity, in which representation is as yet undifferentiated from the movements and actions which make the communion towards which it tends a reality to the group. Their participation in it is so effectively *lived* that it is not yet properly imagined.

This stage is not only pre-logical, but also pre-mythical. It is anterior to collective representations themselves, as I have been using the term. Thus, the first development Durkheim traces is from symbiosis or active participation (where the individual feels he *is* the totem)[1] to collective representations of the totemic type (where the individual feels that his ancestors were the totem, that he will be when he dies, etc.). From this symbolic apprehension he then arrives at the duality, with which we are more familiar, of ideas on the one hand and numinous religion on the other.

This extra-sensory participation of the percipient in the representation involves a similar link between the representations themselves, and of course between one percipient and another. 'Mana' or 'waken' (which *we* can only translate by abstract terms like 'totemic principle', 'life principle' or—since it is present also in inanimate objects—'being') is anterior to the individuality of persons and objects; these (says Durkheim) are rather apprehended by the very primi-

[1] Anyone who finds it difficult to form any conception of participation, that is, of self and not-self identified in the same moment of experience, should reflect on that whole peculiar realm of semi-subjectivity which still leads a precarious existence under the name of 'instinct'—or on those 'irresistible' impulses, on which psychiatrists are inclined to dwell. Many of us know what panic feels like, and ordinary men are proud of their sexual vigour or ashamed of the lack of it, although the act is readily acknowledged in retrospect to be at least as much something that is done to, or with, them by an invisible force of nature, as something they themselves veritably *do*.

tive as 'stopping-places of mana'. It is, incidentally, here that he finds the prototype of the idea of *force*, which played such a prominent part in the physical science of the nineteenth century. And in emphasizing the 'religious origin' of this idea he points out, rather appositely, that Comte regarded the notion of force as a superstition, which was destined to disappear from science—as indeed it has shown marked signs of doing, since Durkheim's book was published.

I hope I have not misrepresented either of the two anthropologists from whom I have quoted rather freely. The more so, as I cannot pause to consider the adverse criticism which Lévy-Bruhl in particular has aroused. (I doubt if it was his case that all primitives *invariably* think in the prelogical way. It is certainly not mine.) If I have drawn heavily on these two writers, I have done so by way of illustration rather than argument. It is not very difficult to see what they mean and, by seeing what they mean, the reader may possibly be helped to see what *I* mean.

Collective representations do not imply a collective unity distinct from the individuals comprising the social group. On the other hand their existence does not derive from the individual. In these two respects they may be compared to language. Like the words of a language, they are common to the members of a given social group, and are transmitted from one generation to another, developing and changing only gradually in the process.

Moreover it is impossible to draw a very precise line between representations and beliefs about representations, or, in the terms I have been using, between figuration and alpha-thinking. All collective representations involve figuration and therefore, if figuration is a kind of thinking, involve 'thought'. But in addition to this nearly all of them involve elements which are actually *apprehended* as thought, or imagined, rather than as perceived. It was this presumably which persuaded Lévy-Bruhl to add the word 'mystic' to his 'participation'. He uses it, he says, 'in the strictly defined sense in which "mystic" implies belief in forces and influences and actions, which though imperceptible to sense, are nevertheless real'.

When I see a stone fall to the ground, do I 'believe' that it is drawn by the force, or the law, of gravity? When I use the telephone, do I 'believe' that my correspondent's voice is recorded and reproduced by an invisible called 'electricity'? Or are both these thoughts immediately experienced in my representation? Or is one so and not the other? The exact point at which a piece of alpha-thinking has slipped into and become an integral part of the representation is hard to determine and may clearly differ somewhat between individuals of the same social group and for the same individual at different times. It is continually happening, while we are growing up, especially while we are learning to speak. I say I 'hear a thrush singing outside my window'. But do I? He is invisible, and it might perhaps be a blackbird; I have begun the business of thinking and believing already! The same thing happens to a lifelong birdwatcher. He does no thinking at all. He *recognizes*. He hears a thrush singing. For him alpha-thinking has become figuration.

To sum up what has been said in this chapter: Anthropology began by assuming as a matter of course that primitive peoples perceive the same phenomena as we do and on that assumption investigated their beliefs about these phenomena. Now however some anthropologists have begun to point out that the difference between the primitive outlook and ours begins at an earlier stage. It is not only a different alpha-thinking but a different figuration, with which we have to do, and therefore the phenomena are treated as collective representations produced by that different figuration. It is further maintained by some of them that the most striking difference between primitive figuration and ours is, that the primitive involves 'participation', that is, an awareness which we no longer have, of an extra-sensory link between the percipient and the representations. This involves, not only that we think differently, but that the

## Participation

phenomena (collective representations) themselves are different. The first three chapters were devoted to reminding the reader that we do, in fact, still participate in the phenomena, though for the most part we do so unconsciously. *We* can only remind ourselves of that participation by beta-thinking and we forget it again as soon as we leave off. This is the fundamental difference, not only between their thinking and ours, but also between their phenomena and ours. It remains to consider how ours, which are genetically the later, have come to pass.

The quotations from Lévy-Bruhl in this chapter are mainly to be found in *Les Fonctions Mentales dans les Sociétés Inférieures* (English Translation: *How Natives Think*). The quotations from Durkheim are all taken from *The Elementary Forms of the Religious Life.*

# V

## PRE-HISTORY

A history of the 'world', as distinct from a history of the
unrepresented, must clearly be a history of phenomena;
that is, of collective representations. But before this part of
the subject is approached, it will be well to consider briefly
the bearing of this truth on what is sometimes called pre-
history. I mean, in particular, the history of the earth before
the appearance on it of human beings.

When particles of rain, rays of light and our watching
eyes are appropriately disposed, we see a rainbow. In the
same way, given the existence of the particles and the presence of human beings on the earth, there arise collective
representations, or in other words the phenomena which we
call 'nature'. When dealing with times in which these conditions were present, therefore, it is quite reasonable to
describe and investigate nature scientifically, not only in the
manner of physics, but also in the manner of the sciences
whose field of study is the past as well as the present, such
as geology, ecology, zoology, and to do this *as if* the phenomena were wholly independent of man's sensory and
psychological participation. It is not necessarily misleading
to do so, and it has proved to be of great practical use. It is
however not sufficiently realized that different considerations apply to any description, in familiar terms, of natural
events and processes deemed to have taken place before the
appearance of human life on the earth.

It may of course be contended (though I should not like

the task) that some animals enjoy representations sufficiently coherent to set up a phenomenal whole, which could be called 'a world' or 'nature'. But this does not really assist much. For, although animals appeared on earth before man, it is certainly not *their* world or nature which geology, for instance, describes; and even so there remains the whole vast panorama of pre-history which is assumed to have preceded the emergence on this planet of sentient life of any description.

Yet by combining, say, biology and geology and omitting physics and physiology, such descriptions are continually offered to us and form, I suppose, a recognized part of the education of most children to-day. It can do no harm to recall occasionally that the prehistoric evolution of the earth, as it is described for example in the early chapters of H. G. Wells's *Outline of History*, was not merely never seen. It never occurred. Something no doubt occurred, and what is really being propounded by such popular writers, and, so far as I am aware, by the text-books on which they rely, is this. That at that time the unrepresented was behaving in such a way that, *if* human beings with the collective representations characteristic of the last few centuries of western civilization had been there, the things described would also have been there.

This is not quite the same thing. It needs, I should have thought, to be considered in connection with another fact, namely, that when attention is *expressly* directed to the history of the unrepresented (as in calculations of the age of the earth based on radio-activity), it is invariably assumed that the behaviour of the unrepresented has remained fundamentally unchanged. Moreover (and this is, to my mind, more important), for those hypothetical 'human beings with collective representations characteristic of the last few centuries of western civilization' we might choose to substitute other human beings—those, for instance, who lived one or two or three or more thousand years ago. We should then have to write a different pre-history altogether.

And we are not entitled to assume without inquiry that, as an indirect means of suggesting the truth about pre-historic goings-on in the unrepresented, such an alternative 'model' would be any less efficient than the one we have in fact chosen. It might be very much more so.

As these consequences may be startling enough to the reader to cause him to reject them, even though he has so far followed me with sympathy, I will, at the risk of repeating myself, put as clearly as I can the alternatives to accepting them. If we refuse to accept them, we can adopt one of three courses, to each of which there are, to me, insuperable objections. We can adopt a sort of super-naïve realism, rejecting all the rigmarole of physics, physiology and psychology with the healthy instinct of Dr. Johnson kicking his stone. 'Nature is nature, and the earth is the earth, and always has been since it all began.' This may do for the present moment, but for a scientifically reconstructed pre-historic past it is open to the objection that, if we are going to reject the reasoned inferences of one set of scientists, there seems no particular reason why we should accept those of another. Or we can resort frankly to 'double-think'. We can think that what physics tells us is true, is true when we are studying physics, and untrue when we are studying something else. The objections to this course are obvious to me, and will be equally so to some of my readers. There are those who will nevertheless continue to adopt it. This book is addressed to the others. Lastly we can adopt a Berkeleyan view of phenomena. For Berkeley held that, not merely the unrepresented, but the representations *as such*, are sustained by God in the absence of human beings. This involves the, for me, too difficult corollary that, out of all the wide variety of collective representations which are found even to-day over the face of the earth, and the still wider variety which history unrolls before us, God has chosen for His delight the particular set shared by Western man in the last few centuries.

It does not of course necessarily follow that all the current descriptions of pre-history are absurd. Even if the usual way of recording what, in the absence of man, was going on in the unrepresented must be criticised as a dubious extrapolation, the descriptions may still, as I have suggested, be valuable, not as actual descriptions, but as notional 'models'. What is important is, to remember that that is all they are. (Especially will this be the case, if we should ever have to assess the merits of this approach against those of any other possible way of acquiring knowledge of the pre-historic past.) For their nature is that of artificial imagery. And when the nature and limitations of artificial images are forgotten, they become idols. Francis Bacon declared that the medieval approach to reality was under the spell of four different sorts of idols, which he called 'idols of the cave', 'idols of the tribe' and so forth. In the same way, these images of what was going on in the unrepresented in the pre-historic past may be called 'idols of the study'. At least that is what they are, if their nature and limitations are forgotten. And I am not sure that as yet these have even been *noticed*.

It is, however, not only these purely theoretical or academic idols with which this book is concerned.

# VI

# ORIGINAL PARTICIPATION

It is characteristic of our phenomena—indeed it is this, above all, which distinguishes them from those of the past —that our participation in them, and therefore also their representational nature, is excluded from our immediate awareness. It is consequently always ignored by our 'common sense' and sometimes denied even in theory. For this reason it will be best to begin the brief series of observations which I want to make upon the history of phenomena— that is, the history of the familiar world—from the present day, and to work backwards from there to the remoter past. Our first step, then, is to trace the last stage of this development, which has led up to the collective representations with which we are familiar to-day.

Participation is the extra-sensory relation between man and the phenomena. It was shown in Chapter III that the existence of phenomena depends on it. Actual participation is therefore as much a fact in our case as in that of primitive man. But we have also seen that we are unaware, whereas the primitive mind is aware of it. This primitive awareness, however, is obviously not the theoretical kind which *we* can still arrive at by beta-thinking. For that presupposes some acquaintance with the findings of modern physics and physiology and can only be applied to the kind of collective representations that go with this. The primitive kind of participation is indeed not theoretical at all, inasmuch as it is given in immediate experience. Let us distinguish it from ours by calling it 'original' participation. It would however be cumbersome to add the epithet every time the word is used and I propose very often to omit it, having first made it plain here and now that by 'participation' I shall mean *original participation*, unless the context otherwise requires.

There is another difference between sophisticated and primitive participation. Hitherto we have spoken of *representations* and of the *unrepresented*; but we have said nothing of any 'represented'. This raises the question whether *representation* was the proper word to use at all, or whether it is merely misleading. If an appearance can properly be called a representation, it will certainly be a representation *of* something. Just as 'the particles', then (the name here chosen for all that is conceived to exist *independently* of consciousness), have also been called the *unrepresented*, so, whatever is *correlative* to the appearances or representations will here be called the *represented*. This is of course a mere name, and gives as yet no clue to the nature of what is meant. I hope that further light will be thrown upon it, gradually, as we proceed. Meanwhile I must use the name, leaving the reader to make up his mind, *ambulando*, whether it was justified or not.

We have seen that a very large part of the collective representations is found by beta-thinking to have been contributed by the percipient's own activity. Beta-thinking therefore inevitably assumes that a very large part of their correlative, the *represented*, is to be found 'within' ourselves. Consequently if *our* participation, having been first understood and accepted, by beta-thinking, as a fact, should then become a conscious experience, it would have to take the form of conscious (instead of, as now, unconscious) figuration. This is because for us, the represented is conceived as within our percipient selves; and it is only the unrepresented physical base ('particles') which we conceive of as without. Not so for primitives. For them the represented, too, is conceived as outside, so that there is no question of conscious figuration. It may also sometimes be detected within, but it is detected primarily without. The human soul may be one of the 'stopping-places' for *mana*, but what differentiates the primitive mind from ours is, that it conceives itself to be only *one* of those stopping-places and not necessarily the most significant. The essence of *original* participation is that there stands behind the phenomena, *and on the other side of them from me*, a represented which is of the same nature as me. Whether it is called 'mana', or by the names of many gods and demons, or God the Father, or the spirit world, it is of the same nature as the perceiving self, inasmuch as it is not mechanical or accidental, but psychic and voluntary.

I have here assumed that what Lévy-Bruhl and Durkheim, and their followers say about contemporary primitive man is substantially correct; and it seems to me likely to be so.[1] But whether or not it is correct for contemporary primitive man, it is certainly true of historically early man. All the evidence from etymology and elsewhere goes to show that the further back we penetrate into the past of human consciousness, the more mythical in their nature do the representations become. Moreover there is no evidence to the contrary. I shall say something later on of the testimony borne by etymology. Here it must suffice to affirm categorically that, for the nineteenth-century fantasy of early man first gazing, with his mind *tabula rasa*, at natural phenomena like ours, then seeking to explain them with thoughts like ours, and then by a process of inference 'peopling' them with the 'aery phantoms' of mythology, there just is not any single shred of evidence whatever.

I do not mean, by using the word 'fantasy', to imply contempt. If great scholars like Max Müller and Sir James Frazer, in seeking for the historical origins of myth, made the same mistake as the early anthropologists, it will, I hope, become apparent in the course of this and the ensuing chapters how inevitable it was that they should do so. To-day, on the other hand, partly thanks to their work, any

[1] Compare, more recently, the last two talks in *The Institutions of Primitive Society* (A series of Broadcast Talks). Blackwell. 1954.

little man, provided he is not hopelessly prejudiced, can convince himself of the contrary. The point is, not to find someone to turn up our noses at, but to grasp the fact that alpha-thinking, when men first began to exercise it, had to be directed upon *that* kind of collective representation (namely the participated kind) and not on collective representations resembling ours, which (as we shall see) are a later product of that very alpha-thinking.

For alpha-thinking, as I have defined it, is a thinking *about* collective representations. But when we think 'about' anything, we must necessarily be aware of ourselves (that is, of the self which is doing the thinking) as sharply and clearly detached from the thing thought about. It follows that alpha-thinking involves *pro tanto* absence of participation. It is in fact the very nature and aim of pure alpha-thinking to exclude participation. When, therefore, it is directed, as it has to be to start with, on phenomena determined by original participation, then, at first simply by being alpha-thinking, and at a later stage deliberately, it seeks to destroy that participation. The more so because (as we shall also see), participation renders the phenomena less predictable and less calculable.

The history of alpha-thinking accordingly includes the history of science, as the term has hitherto been understood, and reaches its culmination in a system of thought which only interests itself in phenomena to the extent that they can be grasped as independent of consciousness. This culmination appears to have been reached about the close of the nineteenth century. For, along with the recent tendency of physics to implicate the observer again in the phenomena, there goes the tendency of physicists to give up alpha-thinking about phenomena and occupy themselves, as mathematicians, only with the unrepresented.

Systematic alpha-thinking appears to have begun with astronomy. Whether this was because the movements of the heavenly bodies display a regularity which is mostly lacking in sublunary phenomena, and which would be the first therefore to attract the attention of minds beginning for the first time to interest themselves in regularity, or whether it was for some other reason, we need not consider. Astronomy is generally regarded as the *doyen* of the sciences, and a glance at its history from Greek times to the present day or thereabouts will afford some insight into the development of that exact thinking about phenomena which is called science and the effect of that development on the collective representations of Western man. I say from Greek times because, although the Egyptians and Chaldeans appear to have kept astronomical records over a very long period, we know nothing of any avowedly *speculative* thought earlier than the Greeks either on this or on any other subject.

That the collective representations to which this speculative thought was applied were of the kind already indicated, i.e. participated, is obvious enough. Apart from speculative thought, it would never have occurred to an ancient Greek to doubt that the heavenly bodies and their spheres were in one way or another representations of divine beings. Such a doubt was, in fact, voiced occasionally—simply because the Greek mind was of such an incorrigibly speculative nature that there was very little that did *not* occur to it—as a purely notional possibility. But the point is that, in the early days of alpha-thinking, any such notion was a secondary speculation, and rather a wild one, about collective representations whose character made the contrary, 'representational', view seem the obvious one.

The systematic alpha-thinking exercised only by the thoughtful few is applied to the phenomena, that is, to collective representations which they share with the many. And we are left in no doubt by Plato's Dialogues, and by the whole language and literature of Greece, what these, in general, were like. There it was the materialist who looked like a Berkeley, and the Greek equivalent of Dr. Johnson would return from speculation to common sense, not by kicking a stone, but by appealing to collective representations made obvious by his upbringing, by the language he

spoke and heard spoken all around him, and by the active
cults which were his daily matter of fact experience. Even
the atoms of Democritus were, of course, not atoms, as the
word has been understood in the nineteenth and twentieth
centuries. They were imagined as components of mind no
less than of matter. In other words they were the only sort
of atoms which alpha-thinking about participated phenomena *could* present to itself for the purpose of speculation.

It is in this light that we must approach, if we wish to
understand them, not only the speculations of Plato, and
Aristotle, for instance, on the nature of the stars and planets,
but also the meanings of common words like *νοῦς* (*nous*)
and *λόγος* (*logos*), and the whole apparatus of language by
which they expressed these speculations. If we are content
to translate, and to *think*, 'mind' for *νοῦς* and 'reason' or
'word' for *λόγος*, we are in continual danger of surrepti-
tiously substituting our own phenomena for those which
they were in fact dealing with. It is not only that they specu-
lated on whether the planets were 'visible gods' or only
images of the gods, as statues are; on the nature of the Fifth
Essence and its relation to the earthly elements; on the
Anima Mundi; on whether or not the Aether, which is the
substance of the spheres, has a soul, etc. The very meanings
of the incidental words with the help of which they did the
speculating, implied participation *of some sort*. Whereas the
words into which we struggle to translate them imply the
reverse. Some examples of these words will be considered
in a later chapter, when it will be seen that original participation survived in an attenuated form even into the
Middle Ages.

It may remove the risk of misunderstanding if I mention
at this early stage that it is no part of the object of this book
to advocate a return to original participation.

# VII

## APPEARANCE AND HYPOTHESIS

According to Plato there were three stages, or degrees of knowledge. The first and lowest amounted to no more than observation. Since all that we perceive is continually changing, coming into being and passing away, this kind of 'knowledge' grasps nothing permanent and nothing therefore which can properly be called 'truth'. At the opposite pole, the highest degree—which is the only one that can *properly* be called knowledge—is wholly extra-sensory. It is the contemplation by pure intelligence of the divine ideas, and above all of the Supreme Good. The union of these two, that is, of pure intelligence and sense-knowledge, gives rise to an intermediate mental activity, which Plato stigmatized as 'bastard'—although he insisted on all his pupils studying it as a preparation and a means to the true knowledge. This intermediate activity was geometry; or, as we should now say, mathematics.

These three degrees of knowledge corresponded with three different levels of astronomy. The astronomy of observation merely records the movements of the stars, the sun, the moon and the planets, without attempting to account for them or reduce them to any system. From this we can rise to the second astronomy, which seeks to account for the apparently arbitrary movement of, for instance, the planets by supposing regular geometrical patterns to underlie them. By the exercise of this celestial geometry we can render ourselves capable of rising eventually to the third and highest, that is, to the only true knowledge; which is an unobscured participation in the divine Mind, or Word, itself. The real wisdom, as distinct from its not wholly unworthy outcome in the permanent truths of geometry, manifests itself only to him who participates in however slight a degree in the pure and divine Intelligence. This intelligent participation, the privilege of philosophy and in the last resort of initiation, was not mystical. For mystical experience is essentially other than ordinary experience. But the Platonic or Aristotelian participation, which was true knowledge, was simply the half-conscious participation of every man (the participation by virtue of which he *was* a man) cleared of the gross and bewildering mutability which is plastered over it by the other approach, through the senses.

Plato further laid it down orally, as we learn from later astronomers, that the science of astronomy proper lay within the middle one of these three spheres of knowledge. In the first place the 'phaenomena', or 'appearances', that is the apparent movements of the heavenly bodies, could be watched by observation. In the third place the true knowledge, since it was acquainted with the divine spirits who ensouled or guided the heavenly bodies, had already laid down certain fundamental principles, not derived from observation. It was for the science of astronomy, in the second place, to 'save' the 'appearances', that is, the apparent movements of the heavenly bodies, and particularly of sun, moon and planets, which were the most difficult to account for, by devising hypothetical patterns of movement, which would account for the appearances without infringing the fundamental principles. Later on, I shall say something of the 'mental-spatial' experience which claimed to determine the nature of movement out of the nature of pure thought. It appears as a mere confusion to the alpha-thinking of to-day (though that, too, is beginning to talk without appreciable discomfort of 'space-time'). Here it must suffice to record that the prescribed movements were, among other requirements, perfect circles at a constant speed.

## Appearance and Hypothesis

There is perhaps more of physics than of astronomy in Aristotle's *De Caelo*, but, as far as the three stages of knowledge and the fundamental principles just referred to are concerned, he was substantially in accord with Plato.

The 'phaenomena' of which the astronomy of Greece and of the dark and middle ages spoke, were of course not quite what we to-day mean by 'phenomena', a word which, outside philosophy, has come to be practically synonymous with 'objects' and 'events'. The middle voice of the Greek verb suggests neither wholly 'what is perceived, from within themselves, by men' nor wholly 'what, from without, forces itself on man's senses', but something between the two. This is also fairly suggested by the English word 'appearances', which is generally used in translating the once hard-worked phrase σώζειν τὰ φαινόμενα—'to save the appearances'. This phrase, used by Simplicius in his sixth century *Commentary* on Aristotle's *De Caelo*, continued to dominate astronomy down to the time of Copernicus.

When we hear of 'saving appearances' to-day, we are apt to think of a society hostess at a dinner party where something has gone wrong in the kitchen. It was not so in the seventeenth century. Although he spoke of God's laughter, Milton was not *himself* laughing at the astronomers when he wrote in the Eighth book of *Paradise Lost*:

> Or if they list to try
> Conjecture, he his fabric of the heavens
> Hath left to their disputes, perhaps to move
> His laughter at their quaint opinions wide
> Hereafter, when they come to model heaven,
> And calculate the stars; how they will wield
> The mighty frame; how build, unbuild, contrive,
> To save appearances; how gird the sphere
> With centric and eccentric scribbled o'er,
> Cycle and epicycle, orb in orb.

Nor was he suggesting that desperate expedients were being resorted to, in order to 'save' (in the sense of rescuing) the

Ptolemaic system—which, incidentally, he had made the framework of his own poem. He was introducing a learned *cliché*.

The same passage from Simplicius contains the Greek verb from which we derive the word 'hypothesis'. The spheres and orbits by which the appearances were to be saved were normally 'hypotheses' in the strict sense of the word, that is, assumptions made for the purpose of a particular argument and by the same token not posited as true. A brief digression on the almost lost distinction between the word 'hypothesis' and the word 'theory' may not be amiss here. The Greek word θεωρία (theoria) meant 'contemplation' and is the term used in Aristotle's psychology to designate the moment of fully conscious participation, in which the soul's *potential* knowledge (its ordinary state) becomes *actual*, so that man can at last claim to be 'awake'. This is no guide to its present, or even recent meaning, but it does emphasize the difference between a proposition which it is hoped may turn out to be true, and a proposition, the truth or untruth of which is irrelevant. The geometrical paths and movements devised for the planets were, in the minds of those who invented them, *hypotheses* in the latter sense. They were arrangements—devices—for saving the appearances; and the Greek and medieval astronomers were not at all disturbed by the fact that the same appearances could be saved by two or more quite different hypotheses, such as an eccentric or an epicycle or, particularly in the case of Venus and Mercury, by supposed revolution round the earth or supposed revolution round the sun. All that mattered was, which was the simplest and the most convenient for practical purposes; for neither of them had any essential part in truth or knowledge.

Unless we realize, with the help of a little historical excavation of this kind, what from the epistemological point of view astronomy then signified and had signified for about two thousand years, we shall not understand the real significance of Copernicus and Galileo. The popular view is, that Copernicus 'discovered' that the earth moves round the sun. Actually the *hypothesis* that the earth revolves round the sun is at least as old as the third century B.C., when it was advanced by Aristarchus of Samos, and he was neither the only, nor probably the first astronomer to think of it. Copernicus himself knew this. Secondly it is generally believed that the Church tried to keep the discovery dark. Actually Copernicus did not himself want to publish his *De Revolutionibus Orbium*, and was only eventually prevailed on to do so by the importunity of two eminent Churchmen.

The real turning-point in the history of astronomy and of science in general was something else altogether. It took place when Copernicus (probably—it cannot be regarded as certain) began to think, and others, like Kepler and Galileo, began to affirm that the heliocentric hypothesis not only saved the appearances, but was physically true. It was this, this novel idea that the Copernican (and therefore any other) hypothesis might not be a hypothesis at all but the ultimate truth, that was almost enough in itself to constitute the 'scientific revolution', of which Professor Butterfield has written:

> it outshines everything since the rise of Christianity and reduces the Renaissance and Reformation to the rank of mere episodes, mere internal displacements, within the system of medieval Christendom.[1]

When the ordinary man hears that the Church told Galileo that he might teach Copernicanism as a hypothesis which saved all the celestial phenomena satisfactorily, but 'not as being the truth', he laughs. But this was really how Ptolemaic astronomy had been taught! In its actual place in history it was not a casuistical quibble; it was the refusal (unjustified it may be) to allow the introduction of a new and momentous doctrine. It was not simply a new theory of the nature of the celestial movements that was feared, but

[1] *Origins of Modern Science*. Bell. 1949. Macmillan. 1951.

a new theory of the nature of theory; namely, that, if a hypothesis saves all the appearances, it is identical with truth.[1]

Geometry, applied to motion, produces the machine. Years ago the Arabs had used the Ptolemaic hypothesis, to make machines or models of the planetary system purely for the purpose of calculation. *Our* collective representations were born when men began to take the models, whether geometrical or mechanical, literally. The machine is geometry in motion, and the new picture of the heavens as a *real* machine, was made possible by parallel developments in physics, where the new theory of inertia (in its early form of 'impetus') assumed, for the first time in the history of the world, that bodies can go on moving indefinitely without an animate or psychic 'mover'. It was soon to be stamped indelibly on men's imaginations by the circumstance of their being ever more and more surrounded by actual artificial machinery on earth. The whole point of a machine is, that, for as long as it goes on moving, it 'goes on by itself' without man's participation. To the extent therefore that the phenomena are experienced as machine, they are believed to exist independently of man, not to be participated and therefore not to be in the nature of representations. We have seen that all these beliefs are fallacious.

All this is not of course to say that science to-day conceives of nature as a machine, or even on a mechanical model. It is to say that the ordinary man has been doing just that for long enough to deprive the phenomena of those last representational overtones—'last enchantments', as Matthew Arnold called them—which still informed them in the Middle Ages, and to eliminate from them the last traces of original participation. In doing so he has produced

[1] Cf. Aquinas, *Summa*, 1a. Qu. 32. a. 1 ad 2. The other view was assumed by Ptolemy himself (*Almagest*, Bk. III, chaps. ii and iv; Bk. XIII, chap. ii). In the time of Copernicus it was still the official view, though not undisputed. See also Note at the end of this Chapter.

the mechanomorphic collective representations which constitute the Western world to-day.

The reader who wishes to verify, or investigate further, the argument of this
Chapter, should consult P. Duhem's *Le Système du Monde. Histoire des doctrines cosmologiques de Platon à Copernic.* Paris 1913–17. This monumental work,
which combines German thoroughness with French lucidity, was unfortunately never finished. The author had completed five (out of, I believe,
eight) volumes before his death. The latest part of the period defined in the
sub-title is, however, covered briefly in a series of articles by Duhem printed
in *Annales de Philosophie Chrétienne* (Apl.–Sept. 1908) under the title Σώζειν
τὰ φαινόμενα. *Essai sur la Notion de Théorie Physique de Platon à Galilée.*

*Le Système du Monde* also gives a full historical account of refinements into
which it would have been disproportionate for me to enter, such as the oppo-
sition of the more literal-minded Arabian astronomers to the Ptolemaic
hypotheses (on the ground of their incompatibility with *Aristotelian* physics)
and the epistemological distinction, at one time sharply emphasized, between
the subject-matter of physics (sublunary phenomena) and astronomy (celestial
phenomena).

See also *Aquinas and Kant* by Gavin Ardley. Longmans Green & Co. 1950.

# VIII

## TECHNOLOGY AND TRUTH

We have just distinguished between the actual doctrines of modern science and the collective representations to which the growth of science has contributed. Thus, on the one hand attention may be directed to the history of alpha-thinking itself—what is ordinarily called the history of thought or the history of ideas. On the other hand it may be turned to the *effects* of an alpha-thinking which has continued long and widely enough to pass over into figuration, and be, as it were, smitten into the representations themselves; that is part of the history of *consciousness*, and of the collective representations which are its correlative. Now although my subject is not the doctrines of science, but rather the collective representations, which have been so deeply affected by the doctrines of science, it may be well to pause here for a moment and consider the relation of scientific theories to truth and knowledge.

What is the view taken by scientists themselves of that relation? The answer is not very clear. And it is a good deal less clear to-day than it was a generation ago. The limited scope of all scientific inquiry is to-day often emphasized rather strongly by those engaged in it. So much so, that when we have heard them on the subject, we are sometimes left with the feeling that we ought to look on all scientific theories as mere 'hypotheses' in the sense of the Platonic and medieval astronomers, and that it is wrong to take any of them with the 'literalness' that embroiled Galileo with the

Church. They are at best, we are assured, the mathematical formulae which up to the time of writing have been found the simplest and most convenient for—well, for saving the appearances. In physics in particular there is a marked tendency to treat almost as an *enfant terrible* anyone who takes the models literally enough to refer to them in any context outside that of physical inquiry itself.[1] It would seem to follow from this that, as Plato and the astronomers believed, scientific hypotheses have no direct relation to the real nature of things.

On the other hand I find something equivocal in the public utterances of the spokesmen of science. For the same ones who have just been stressing this unpretentious view of scientific theory will frequently let drop some such phrase as 'some day we may know'—or even 'we now know'—when speaking, not of some particular hypothesis, but of quite general conclusions about the nature of universe, earth or man. Moreover, if the occasion is a formal one, we often get some reference to the history of science, in terms of 'advancing the frontiers of knowledge', and so forth. All this indicates a very different conception of science and strongly suggests to the audience that modern science, so far from being disentitled to claim the status of knowledge, is the only reliable knowledge available to us. At the least, it suggests that the findings of any particular science are not merely tools for the application and further pursuit of that science, but have some sort of absolute validity.

Perhaps the confusion is at present unavoidable, but let us at least be clear that it *is* a confusion between two quite incompatible views. Let us see, for instance, what consequences flow from adopting the first view, namely, that scientific theories are simply hypotheses to save the appearances. This can best be done with the help of a grotesquely over-simplified analogy. But first let me make the bearing of the analogy clear. It will contrast two different sorts of

[1] Anyone, it has been said, may ask questions concerning wave-mechanics; but only cads talk about 'ether'!

'knowledge', both of which, *in the analogy*, depend on alpha-thinking; but it will *illustrate* the difference between a 'knowledge' which does depend on alpha-thinking and a different kind of knowledge altogether which does not. Plato and Aristotle, and others, as we have seen, taught that there was such a knowledge and that it was accessible only to participation. But it is not necessary to believe this in order to understand the analogy.

Take a clever boy, who knows nothing about the principle of internal combustion or the inside of an engine, and leave him inside a motor-car, first telling him to move the various knobs, switches and levers about and see what happens. If no disaster supervenes, he will end by finding himself able to drive the car. It will then be true to say that he knows *how to drive* the car; but untrue to say that he knows the car. As to that, the most we could say would be that he has an 'operative' knowledge of it—because for operation all that is required is a good empirical acquaintance with the dashboard and the pedals. Whatever we say, it is obvious that what he has is very different from the knowledge of someone else, who has studied mechanics, internal combustion and the construction of motor-cars, though he has perhaps never driven a car in his life, and is perhaps too nervous to try. Now whether or no there is another kind of knowledge of nature, which corresponds to 'engine-knowledge' in the analogy, it seems that, *if the first view of the nature of scientific theory is accepted*, the *kind* of knowledge aimed at by science must be, in effect, what I will call 'dashboard-knowledge'.

Francis Bacon, whose startlingly original mind was so influential in bringing about the scientific revolution, was very frank about this. Not only did he maintain that knowledge was to be valued for the *power* it gives man over nature; but he practically made success in this aim a part of his definition of knowledge. The key words he uses to distinguish the knowledge he exalts from the knowledge pursued by the Schoolmen are 'fruit' and 'operation'. In other words, not only 'science' but knowledge itself, that is, the only knowledge that is not mere trifling, is, for him—technology. Knowledge (for which Bacon, when he wrote in Latin, of course used the word *scientia*) is that which enables us to make nature do our bidding.

I think it must be acknowledged that the 'idea' which stands behind the particular kind of knowledge which we have come to call 'science' is 'dashboard-knowledge'. I mean only that that is its *mode* of 'knowing'. I do not of course mean that the motive by which the great scientists have been inspired has been the desire for power. The analogy is admittedly a crude one. For, while the dashboard of even the most expensive and up-to-date car is a comparatively simple affair, nature's 'dashboard'—that is, her exterior, accessible to the senses and the reason—is of such a marvellous and intricate complexity that many a man has counted his life well spent in mastering a tiny corner of it.

If however it *is* acknowledged, what follows? If science is merely technology, if the theories of physics in particular are mere hypotheses to save the appearances, with no necessary relation to ultimate truth, then—well, in the first place, one hopes that the car will not break down. But, in the second place, it might be argued that they should be consistently treated as such. It might be said that the theories of physics should be reserved for the purposes of physics and left out of sight altogether, when we are thinking about anything else—about the nature of perception, for instance. This would remove the foundation from under the first part of this book. But it would also have so many other, and such startling consequences, that I am not seriously alarmed.

For, in the first place, we could not limit the new and more hypothetical way of thinking to nuclear, or recent physics. The laws of gravity, for example, and of inertia, must go the same way as the electrons, as far as any ultimate validity is concerned. Secondly, you cannot really isolate one science from others in this way, nor is it the practice to do so. One has only to think of the effects of physical theory, treated as fact, on the sciences of medicine and astronomy as exemplified in radio-therapy and astrophysics. Thirdly, and most important of all for my purposes, the hypotheses do in fact, get into the collective representations;[1] many of them are, and others soon may be, implicit in the very 'nature' which surrounds us, and therefore in the world in which I have to write. And lastly the withdrawal from 'participation', which alpha-thinking has brought about, has its advantages. The vagaries of confusion and savagery in the tribes in which anthropology finds participation most conspicuously surviving to-day, though they may well not be very reliable guides to its ancient quality among other peoples who have long since abandoned it, do nevertheless remind us of the sins of commission in thought, feeling and action of which original participation is capable. Whatever sins of omission alpha-thinking may be guilty of, we owe to it, up to now, our independence, much of our security, our psychological integrity and perhaps our very existence as individuals. When Prospero renounced his last enchantments and set sail for civilization, Ariel, it is true, remained with Caliban—but so did Setebos.

Apart from all this, there is one conclusive reason why, in spite of the technological slant of natural science, our beta-thinking is bound to *begin* with the assumption that alpha-thinking has a valid relation to truth. With collective representations like ours, what else can we do? Where else can we start from? If the physical theory of an unrepresented base *has* some such validity, so much the better. If not—even if it amounts to positive error—the way out may still lie through and not back. The best way of escape from deep-rooted error has often proved to be, to pursue it to its logical conclusion, that is, to go on taking it seriously and see what follows. Only we must be consistent. We must take it *really* seriously. We must give up double-think. For inconsistent and slovenly thought can abide indefinitely in error without any feeling of discomfort.

[1] Cf. pp. 51 and 53.

# IX

## AN EVOLUTION OF IDOLS

It is the common opinion that, whereas we see nature pretty much as she really is, primitive man sees and archaic or early man saw her all awry through the veil of a complicated system of fancies and beliefs. If, however, the general conclusions of Chapter IV are accepted, it is clear that, whether or no archaic man saw nature awry, what he saw was not primarily determined by *beliefs*. On the other hand it was suggested in Chapter VII that what *we* see *is* so determined. If I am right therefore, there is indeed a contrast between primitive and modern consciousness and that contrast *is* connected with beliefs, but in exactly the opposite way to what is generally supposed. Precisely what beliefs about phenomena have been widely and confidently and long enough held to become actually part of a representation, is, as I have said, a matter on which opinions may well differ in any particular case. But, whether they are part of our collective representations or not, it is a fact that there are certain beliefs not only about the structure, but also about the history, of the phenomena surrounding them, which are widely, indeed almost universally, shared by civilized men in this second half of the twentieth century. There are also beliefs, only a little less confidently and a little less universally held, about the history of consciousness. As both these sets of beliefs run sharply counter to a good deal of what I have said and intend to say on the same subject, it will be well to give some indication of how and why these (in my view) mistaken beliefs arose.

But first of all, one more brief digression on the subject of science. Most of what I have said about it has connoted the experimental and practical category. Whether the theories of physics and astronomy, for instance, are truths or approximate truths, or whether they are mere hypotheses to save the appearances, the impressive thing about them is that they *work*. We predict the result of an experiment, we make the experiment, with all adequate safeguards, and the prediction is verified. In the case of astronomy, although we cannot experiment, we can still predict and, in doing so, test the efficiency of our hypotheses.

> They predict many years ahead eclipses of the sun and moon; they specify the day, the hour and the extent; and their reckoning is correct—the events follow their predictions; they have discovered and recorded rules, by which it can be foretold in what year, in what month of the year, on what day of the month, at what hour of the day, in what part of their light the sun and moon are to be eclipsed; and what is foretold occurs.

These words are of course not less, but much more true of the Copernican and Newtonian hypotheses of to-day than they were of the Ptolemaic and contemporary hypotheses to which St. Augustine was referring when he wrote them in his *Confessions*[1] at about the end of the fourth century A.D. By their 'fruits', as Bacon would have said, we know them.

But there are to-day, alongside the practical and experimental sciences, a number of others which are, it seems to me, in a much less happy position. I suppose a large part of astrophysics, for example, to be unverifiable by any prediction or experiment; but I am concerned here more with sciences such as palaeontology and a good part of geology and zoology, whose subject-matter is the past, which naturally cannot be predicted and is not either susceptible of

[1] Bk. V, ch. iii.

experiment. Here we cannot say, with Bacon, 'never mind what those tedious old fools, the Schoolmen, meant by "knowledge"; does it deliver the goods?'. For the only goods to be delivered *are*—knowledge. There is no 'operation', no 'fruit' and no empirical test of accuracy. If *their* hypotheses are not also the actual truth, they are nothing.

It seems to me that the only thing which such purely theoretical sciences really have in common with those at the technological end of the scale, is the healthy *discipline*, the open-minded attitude to fact which is, or should be, common to all whose object is knowledge, and which has itself become so much better understood and acknowledged as a result of the systematic pursuit of empirical science. But it also seems to me that they have in fact borrowed very much more than this. They have for instance accepted many of the hypotheses of sister sciences as established facts, according to them the same status in the construction of their theories as to their own first-hand observation. In this connection I have already pointed out in Chapter V that they have accepted *some* of these hypotheses, while choosing to ignore others. They have moreover borrowed half the vocabulary of hypothesis and empirical verification and are deeply coloured by the technological mode of knowledge which that implies, though it is really quite inappropriate to them. It is almost as if they expected dashboard-knowledge to tell us how the engine was made. I believe this to be one of the reasons, though not the most important one, for the hypothetical picture of the evolution of the earth and man which began at about the end of the eighteenth century to fasten itself on men's minds and which is to-day regarded by ordinary men (as are all but the most recent and avowedly tentative of scientific hypotheses) as palpable fact; which indeed, it may be argued, has become part of their collective representations.

At the beginning of the eighteenth century the variety of natural species was normally attributed by the botany and zoology of the day to supernatural and instantaneous creation. The eighteenth and nineteenth centuries witnessed the almost total disappearance of this tradition, reflected as it was in the elaborately classifying botany of Linnaeus, in favour of a gradual 'evolution'. In the record of the rocks and the dovetailed panorama of organic nature, history and science together gradually divined the vestiges of a different, a 'natural' kind of creation, and one that was the reverse of instantaneous. Nature herself came to be seen as a process in time and the individual phenomena at any moment, instead of being fixed and parallel shapes repeated and repeated since creation's day, were cross-sections of their own development and metamorphosis. They could be truly grasped only by looking before and after. A consideration of the incidental effect of this on our whole conception of the significance of history, and indeed of time itself, must be deferred to a later chapter. Suffice it here to say that the upheaval was all the greater—indeed it amounted in the end to something like an explosion—because it came at a time when the mind of Europe was perhaps more disinclined to look *forward* than at any time in its history. The backward-looking mood of the Revival of Learning had not yet died away and most men were much less concerned with the shape of things to come than with the greatness and wisdom of the ancient Greeks and Romans and the virtues of the noble savage, corrupted (it was held) by the advance of civilization.

In this chapter we are concerned with the form which the hypothesis ultimately took and its effect on the collective representations. This was naturally determined to a large extent by the existing representations to which it was applied. What were the phenomena of nature at the time when the new doctrine began to take effect, and particularly at the Darwinian moment in the middle of the nineteenth century? They were *objects*. They were unparticipated to a degree which has never been surpassed before or since. The habit, begun by the scientific revolution, of regarding the mechanical model constructed by alpha-thinking as the actual and exclusive structure of the universe, had sunk right into them. Hardy's rustics may indeed remind us that change did not proceed everywhere at the same rate even in the English-speaking world; but for townsmen at least—in a world which was already rapidly and is now more rapidly still becoming totally urbanized—the last flicker of medieval participation had died away. Matter and force were enough. There was as yet no thought of an unrepresented base; for if the particles kept growing smaller and smaller, there would always be bigger and better glasses to see them through. The collapse of the mechanical model was not yet in sight, nor had any of those other factors which have since contributed to the passing of the dead-centre of 'literalness'—idealist philosophies, genetic psychology, psycho-analysis—as yet begun to take effect. Consequently there was as yet no dawning apprehension that the phenomena of the familiar world may be 'representations' in the final sense of being the mental construct of the observer. Literalness reigned supreme.

What then had alpha-thinking achieved at precisely this point in the history of the West? It had temporarily set up the appearances of the familiar world (which the same thinking, pursued a little farther—pursued to the point which I have called 'beta'—discovers to be so inextricably involved with man himself) as things wholly independent of man. It had clothed them with the independence and extrinsicality of the unrepresented itself. But a representation, which is collectively mistaken for an ultimate—ought not to be called a representation. It is an idol. Thus the phenomena *themselves* are idols, when they are imagined as enjoying that independence of human perception which can in fact only pertain to the unrepresented. If that is, for the most part, what our collective representations are to-day, it is even more certainly what they were in the second half of the nineteenth century. And it was to *these* collective representations that the evolutionists had to apply their alpha-thinking, just as it was to the quite different representations of their own contemporaries that Plato and Aristotle had to apply theirs. Is it to be wondered at that the evolution which the former have depicted is not a real evolution of phenomena at all, but, as was pointed out in Chapter V, a factitious extrapolation—an evolution of 'idols of the study'?

I am speaking of course of the form which the theory finally took, not of the concept of evolution itself. That is factual enough. The record of the rocks *is* a script containing stored memories of earth's past. It is only a question of how the script is to be read. A touch of that participation which still linked the Greeks, and even the medieval observer with his phenomena, might well have led to a very different interpretation—as it did in the case of Goethe, who had that touch. But for the generality of men, participation was dead; the only link with the phenomena was through the senses; and they could no longer conceive of any manner in which either growth itself or the metamorphoses of individual and special growth, could be determined from within. The appearances were idols. They had no 'within'. Therefore the evolution which had produced them could only be conceived mechanomorphically as a series of impacts of idols on other idols.

If the impulse to construe as process the record of the rocks and the vestiges of creation apparent in the natural order had come either a little earlier, before participation had faded, or a little later, when the iconoclasm implicit in physical analysis—and in the beta-thinking to which it can give rise—had really begun to work, man might have read there the story of the coming into being, *pari passu*, of his world and his own consciousness. As it was, all that palaeontology could take over from the experimental sciences, such as astronomy and physics, was the idols which these latter had so far succeeded in creating. Working with these, it attempted moreover to adopt the orthodox 'geometrizing' tradition of those sciences with a slavishness that led, in one instance at least, to results whose absurdity is only just beginning to dawn on us.

# An Evolution of Idols

There is no more striking example than the Darwinian theory of that borrowing from the experimental by the non-experimental sciences, to which I referred at the beginning of this chapter. It was found that the appearances on earth so much lack the regularity of the appearances in the sky that no systematic hypothesis will fit them. But astronomy and physics had taught men that the business of science is to find hypotheses to save the appearances. By a hypothesis, then, these earthly appearances must be saved; and saved they were by the hypothesis of—chance variation. Now the concept of chance is precisely what a hypothesis is devised to save us from. Chance, in fact, = no hypothesis. Yet so hypnotic, at this moment in history, was the influence of the idols and of the special mode of thought which had begotten them, that only a few—and their voices soon died away—were troubled by the fact that the impressive vocabulary of technological investigation was actually being used to denote its breakdown; as though, because it is something we can do with ourselves in the water, drowning should be included as one of the different ways of swimming.

# X

# THE EVOLUTION OF PHENOMENA

I shall have succeeded very poorly with the opening
chapters of this book, if I have not succeeded in making one
thing plain. It is only necessary to take the first feeble step
towards a renewal of participation—that is, the bare
acknowledgement in beta-thinking that phenomena are
collective representations—in order to see that the actual
evolution of the earth we know must have been at the same
time an evolution of consciousness. For consciousness is correlative to phenomenon. Any other picture we may form
of evolution amounts to no more than a symbolical way of
depicting changes in the unrepresented. Yet curiously
enough, as already observed, this latter kind of evolution is
just what is assumed *not* to have taken place. We look at a
fossil-bearing rock and prove how things have changed by
describing appearances which can never have appeared,
unless there was at the same time consciousness. We fix
the date of those appearances, and exclude the possibility
of consciousness, by measuring the radio-active content
of the rock, on the footing that the behaviour of the
unrepresented has remained unchanged for millions of
years.

By treating the phenomena of nature as objects wholly
extrinsic to man, with an origin and evolution of their own
independent of man's evolution and origin, and then by
endeavouring to deal with these objects as astronomy deals
with the celestial appearances or physics with the particles,

nineteenth-century science, and nineteenth-century speculation, succeeded in imprinting on the minds and imaginations of men their picture of an evolution of idols. One
result of this has been to distort very violently our conception of the evolution of human consciousness. Or rather it
has caused us virtually to deny such an evolution in the face
of what must otherwise have been accepted as unmistakable
evidence.

For the biological picture of evolution was imprinted, no
less deeply than on other men's, on the minds of those
scholars—etymologists, mythologists, anthropologists—
who made it their business to study the human past, and it
was accepted by them, not as speculation or hypothesis, but
as established fact. It was the given framework into which
they had to fit any theory they chose to form. It was treated
as part of the appearances they were setting out to save.
Consequently, in their endeavours to explain the mind of
early or of primitive man, they set him down, in fancy, in
front of phenomena identical with their own, but with his
mind *tabula rasa*, and supposed the origin of human consciousness to lie in his first efforts to speculate about those
phenomena. In this way was evolved the doctrine of
'animism', according to which the fancy of primitive man
had 'peopled' nature with spirits. Now, in order that nature
may be peopled with spirits, nature must first be devoid of
spirit; but this caused the scholars no difficulty, because they
never supposed the possibility of any other kind of nature.
The development of human consciousness was thus presented as a history of alpha-thinking beginning from zero
and applied always to the same phenomena, at first in the
form of erroneous beliefs about them and, as time went on,
in the form of more and more correct and scientific beliefs.
In short, the evolution of human consciousness was reduced
to a bare history of ideas. No doubt the history of consciousness does include the story of any number of erroneous
beliefs, but the erroneous beliefs of human beings about
phenomena are neither the most interesting nor the most

important thing about the human beings or about the phenomena.

It may be objected that what I have recounted in the last three chapters is itself very like a history of ideas and beliefs. This is quite true. It had to be what it was, because I wished to begin by showing how our *present* collective representations arose, and it is just a fact that these are determined by ideas and beliefs rather than—as is the case with participating consciousness—productive of them. At the same time it does raise an important question. Granted that for the past two or three thousand years the process of evolution has consisted in the gradual ousting of participation by alpha-thinking, is even the history of alpha-thinking itself just a history of thought in the ordinary sense, or can we also detect in it the subliminal working of an evolutionary process? A history of thought, as such, amounts to a dialectical or syllogistic process, the thoughts of one age arising discursively out of, challenging, and modifying the thoughts and discoveries of the previous one. Is this all we mean by the history of alpha-thinking?

The evidence points in the opposite direction. Many indications suggest that, in addition to the dialectical history of ideas, there are forces at work beneath the threshold of argument in the evolution even of modern consciousness. Go far enough back and it is obvious. The comparatively sudden appearance, after millennia of static civilizations of the oriental type, of the people or the impulse which eventually flowered in the cultures of the Aryan nations can hardly have been due to the impact of notion on notion. And the same is true of the abrupt emergence at a certain point in history of vociferously speculative thought among the Greeks. Still more remarkable is the historically unfathered impulse of the Jewish nation to set about eliminating participation by quite other methods than those of alpha-thinking. Suddenly, and as it were without warning, we are confronted by a fierce and warlike nation, for whom it is a paramount moral obligation to refrain from the participatory heathen cults by which they were surrounded on all sides; for whom moreover precisely that moral obligation is conceived as the very foundation of the race, the very marrow of its being. We owe to the Jews the pejorative significance in the word *idol*. The representative images, the totemic *eidola*, which ritually focused the participation of the surrounding Gentile nations, are either condemned by their prophets as evil, or denied as unrealities; as when the Psalmist sings:

> Their idols are silver and gold: even the work of men's hands.
> They have mouths, and speak not: eyes have they and see not.
> They have ears, and hear not: noses have they, and smell not.
> They have hands, and handle not; feet have they, and walk not: neither speak they through their throat.

To this I shall return later.

But even when we come to the last seven-leagued step in the development of our modern mechanomorphic consciousness, which occurred at a time when alpha-thinking was already far advanced, we are forced to the same conclusion. Why should the scientific revolution have occurred when it did, and at no other time, although men had been busy saving the appearances by abstract hypotheses for century after century? We might be tempted to answer this question by saying that it came when alpha-thinking had succeeded in developing more efficient instruments of observation, so that observation of the phenomena themselves became at last a viable and more attractive alternative to the traditional medieval practice of merely glossing Aristotle. The scientific revolution, it is often suggested, came about because men began at last to look at nature for themselves and see what happened; and we are referred to Galileo's telescope and Jupiter's moons. But this will hardly suffice. For although post-Copernican astronomy certainly was based on more and better first-hand observation than the old astronomy, yet in the case of physics, as Professor Butterfield has pointed out, it was the other way about. A very long step—and a very difficult one—was taken in the final ousting of participation, when the Aristotelian and medieval doctrine that all bodies come to rest, unless they are kept in motion by a 'mover', was at last abandoned. Yet if we base our hypotheses on the behaviour of the bodies we actually see in motion, this is the only conclusion we can possibly come to. The theory of 'impetus', which later developed into the concept of 'inertia', requires, not observation, but the abstract, geometrizing supposition, never realized in practice—at least on earth—of bodies moving through a gravity-free, frictionless vacuum. In this case therefore the change of outlook—and there could hardly be a more significant one—must have been hindered rather than helped by observation.

No. Although alpha-thinking is itself dialectical, I do not think it can be convincingly maintained that the historical development of alpha-thinking is a purely dialectical process. The evidence in such matters is naturally not of the sort that can be measured with a slide-rule or broken with a hammer, but it does not require all that fineness of perception to discern *behind* the evolution of consciousness the operation of forces beneath its threshold. There is some internal evidence, too. Men concerned with the development of any branch of thought, if they happen also to be acutely conscious of the workings of their own minds, are sometimes surprised at the ease and the force with which ideas tending in a certain direction have come into them. They have been known to speak, not without a kind of bewilderment, of certain thoughts being 'in the air'. The following passage from the *Autobiography* of John Stuart Mill appears to record just such an experience:

What thus impressed me was the chapter in which Bentham passed judgment on the common modes of reasoning in morals and legislation, deduced from phrases like 'law of nature', 'right reason', 'the moral sense', 'natural rectitude', and the like and characterized them as dogmatism in disguise, imposing its sentiments upon others under cover of sounding expressions which convey no reason for the sentiment, but set up the sentiment as its own reason. . . . *The feeling rushed upon me*, that all previous moralists were superseded, and that here indeed was the commencement of a new era in thought.

The italics are mine, but the sentiments are those of that least excitable of men, John Stuart Mill. I quote them only because of the strong feeling I had, when I read them, that here, where one would most of all expect the development of thought to be simply the process of its own discourse, something else was going on underneath it. We must defer until nearer the end any consideration of what that something may be.

# XI

# MEDIEVAL ENVIRONMENT

When the distinction has been appreciated between (1) an imputed evolution of some wholly 'objective', and therefore wholly unrepresented base, (2) a fancied evolution of idols, and (3) the actual evolution of phenomena (including, as that does, a correlative evolution of consciousness), we may be compelled to revise some of our ideas on the amount of time required for the process. It follows, for instance, from what was said in Chapter V, that the period during which the *phenomenal* earth has been evolving is probably much shorter than is now generally assumed. Another consequence is, that evolutionary changes are not purely biological, and that they are not limited to pre-history, but can be detected even in the relatively recent period for which historical records, or indications of some sort, are still available to us. They include changes subtler in their nature and observable over a different time-scale altogether, changes measurable by centuries rather than millennia, and by millennia rather than aeons.

It has already been suggested that the last of these changes occupied only the three or four hundred years which divide our own epoch from the one which preceded the scientific revolution. For this suggestion was implied throughout, in the attempt which was made in Chapters VI and VII to trace the coming into being of our own collective representations. It is now the task of this book to demonstrate in rather more detail, if that be possible, that the men of the middle ages, and their predecessors, did indeed live in a different world from ours. The difficulties in the way of such a demonstration are very great, because, as I have pointed out, it is the very nature of our own representations that they are fixed, as a sort of idols to which all representative significance is denied, and which cannot therefore (so it is felt) have altered merely with the alteration of human consciousness. Since it is, for us, a matter of 'common sense', if not of definition, that phenomena are wholly independent of consciousness, the impulse to ignore or explain away any evidence to the contrary is almost irresistible.

Yet, as with most inveterate prejudices, the reward of overcoming it requites the exertion. The idols are tough and hard to crack, but through the first real fissure we make in them we find ourselves looking, how deeply, into a new world! If the eighteenth-century botanist, looking for the first time through the old idols of Linnaeus's fixed and timeless classification into the new perspective of biological evolution, felt a sense of liberation and of light, it can have been but a candle-flame compared with the first glimpse we now get of the familiar world and human history lying together, bathed in the light of the evolution of consciousness.

That, in a colloquial or metaphorical sense, the man of the middle ages lived in 'a different world' from ours, is obvious enough from the record. Half an hour spent with the illuminated manuscripts in the British Museum would be enough to convince anyone of this, even if there were no cathedrals, no Mystery plays, no frescoes, no heraldry, no psychomachies, no Virgil legend, no Divine Comedy still surviving. But we have here not merely to notice the fact that medieval man expressed himself in so different a manner and in such different terms from those which are natural to us, but to ask the question *why* he did so. Besides producing representations in perception and memory, men reproduce them in their language and art; it is, indeed, in this way that the representations become collective. Through language and traditional art we come without effort to share in the collective representations of our own age and our own community. But where we are concerned with those of an alien or a vanished community, we cannot bring ourselves to the point of sharing them without making an unwonted effort. We have to try to experience them as vitally *as if* they were ours—but our own keep on getting in the way.

The first obvious impression which the art and literature of the Middle Ages make upon us is one of 'quaintness'—that quaintness which disgusted the eighteenth and fascinated the nineteenth century. If we go farther and ask in what this quaintness consists, I think we shall find that it arises, above all, from their combining and, as we should say, confusing two ways of approaching phenomena; ways which we are accustomed to regard as quite distinct from one another. These are the literal, on the one hand, and the symbolic or metaphorical, on the other. In their art, for instance, they felt none of the awkwardness we do about representing invisible or spiritual events and circumstances by material means. The same human figures, costumes, artefacts, etc., could be used in the same picture or carving as literal reproductions of the physical world and as representations of a spiritual world. A farm cart would do for Elijah's fiery chariot on its way up to heaven—and look at any fresco of the Last Judgment.

In the eighteenth and nineteenth centuries men who wanted to paint or sculpt an angel, for instance, or a departed spirit, felt obliged to supply him with a special, unearthly costume—often rather like a nightgown. But *then* there seemed nothing incongruous in using the garments of every day. Certainly, in both periods, angels were often represented with wings, but this really only emphasizes the difference—for they would add wings to the ordinary human figure ordinarily attired, whereas it would clearly be aesthetically impossible and theologically a joke in bad taste to attach wings to a lounge suit. It may be suggested that there is a very simple explanation, namely that lounge suits are 'prosaic', whereas armour, tabards and hose are not. But this is no explanation at all, unless we can also say what we mean by 'prosaic', and therefore *why* our clothes are prosaic, whereas medieval clothes were not. If we cannot, then we are merely left with another form of the same statement. A prosaic object, in other words, is a non-representational one; and our clothes are prosaic, because our minds are literal.

It is very important to realize that, when it is said that the man of medieval and earlier times confused the literal and symbolical approach, what is meant is, that he confused or rather combined the two states of mind *which we to-day mean by those words*. Indeed, we shall find throughout that the main difficulty that prevents us from breaking through the idols to the actuality of history, that is, to the evolution of consciousness, lies in the fact that we go on using the same words without realizing how their meanings have shifted. Thus, exceptional men did sometimes distinguish between the literal and the symbolical use of words and images before the scientific revolution. On the question of hell, for instance, John Scotus Erigena distinguished in the seventh century between the symbol and the symbolized or the representation and the represented, emphasizing that the sufferings of hell are purely spiritual, and that they are described physically for the benefit of simple understandings. The point I am making is that, precisely to those simple understandings, the 'physical' and 'literal' themselves were not what 'physical' and 'literal' are to us. Rather, the phenomena themselves carried the sort of multiple significance which we to-day only find in symbols. Accordingly, the issue, in a given case, between a literal and a symbolical interpretation, though it could be raised, had not the same sharpness as of contradictories. Later, as the representations hardened into idols, the distinction between the two grew sharper and sharper until, in the nineteenth century, the strain of a 'literal' interpretation became intolerable even to simple understandings, and the notion of, for instance, a 'physical' hell was decisively rejected as an impossible superstition. And so indeed it is, if by 'physical' we mean the idols of which our physical world to-day consists. 'Who now believes,' inquired F. C. Conybeare in 1910, 'in a God who has a right and a left hand?'[1]

When the 'things' of the physical world have become idols, then indeed the literal interpretation excludes the symbolical, and *vice versa*. But where every thing is a representation, at least half-consciously experienced as such, there is as yet no such contradiction. For a representation experienced as such is neither literal nor symbolical; or, alternatively, it is both at the same time. Nothing is easier for us, than to grasp a purely literal meaning; and if we are capable at all of grasping, in addition, a symbolical or 'fancy' meaning, as we do in poetry, we are in no danger of confusing the one with the other.[2] Before the scientific revolution, on the other hand, it was the concept of the 'merely literal' that was difficult. And therefore the writer who is referred to as Dionysius the Areopagite, and Thomas Aquinas and others after him, emphasized the importance of using the humblest and most banal images, as symbols for purely spiritual truths or beings. For only in this way could a representation be safely polarized into symbol and symbolized, into literal and metaphorical.

We have seen that phenomena are experienced collectively *as* representations, and not as idols, where there is a survival of participation. In attempting to show that, right down to the period which ended with the scientific revolution, there was such a survival, I can do no more than give a few selected indications. The reader must go elsewhere for a full and detailed account of the medieval outlook.

Since participation is a *way* of experiencing the world in immediacy, and not a system of ideas about experience, or about the world, we obviously shall not find any contemporary *description* of it. When we come to contemporary

---

[1] *Myth, Magic and Morals.*

[2] The meaning, for instance, of the word *garden* in the line: *There is a garden in her face*, is unlikely to be mistaken for the literal meaning.

philosophy and theories of knowledge, we shall indeed find explicit *reference* to participation, but for the moment we are concerned with the ordinary man's experience and not with what philosophers thought about that experience. Contemporary books were written, and contemporary science was expounded, for people assumed to share the collective representations of the writer, and accordingly our evidence must be sought more often in what is implied or assumed than in what is actually affirmed. We can only reconstruct the collective representations of another age obliquely.

Let us make the attempt for a moment. Let us try to place ourselves inside the skin of a medieval 'man in the street', and imagine ourselves looking out at the world through his eyes and thinking about it—not speculating, but thinking ordinary habitual thoughts—with his mind. We are not concerned with what he believed as an obligation of faith or a point of doctrine remote from experience. We are concerned with the sort of thing he took for granted.

To begin with, we will look at the sky. We do not see it as empty space, for we know very well that a vacuum is something that nature does not allow, any more than she allows bodies to fall upwards. If it is daytime, we see the air filled with light proceeding from a living sun, rather as our own flesh is filled with blood proceeding from a living heart. If it is night-time, we do not merely see a plain, homogeneous vault pricked with separate points of light, but a regional, qualitative sky, from which first of all the different sections of the great zodiacal belt, and secondly the planets and the moon (each of which is embedded in its own revolving crystal sphere) are raying down their complex influences upon the earth, its metals, its plants, its animals and its men and women, including ourselves. We take it for granted that those invisible spheres are giving forth an inaudible music—the spheres, not the individual stars (as Shakespeare's Lorenzo instructed Jessica, much later, when the representation had already begun to turn into a vague superstition). As to the planets themselves, without being specially interested in astrology, we know very well that growing things are specially beholden to the moon, that gold and silver draw their virtue from sun and moon respectively, copper from Venus, iron from Mars, lead from Saturn. And that our own health and temperament are joined by invisible threads to these heavenly bodies we are looking at. We probably do not spend any time thinking about these extra-sensory links between ourselves and the phenomena. We merely take them for granted.

We turn our eyes on the sea—and at once we are aware that we are looking at one of the four elements, of which all things on earth are composed, including our own bodies. We take it for granted that these elements have invisible constituents, for, as to that part of them which is incorporated in our own bodies, we experience them inwardly as the four 'humours' which go to make up our temperament. (To-day we still catch the lingering echo of this participation, when Shakespeare makes Mark Antony say of Brutus:

> . . . The elements
> So mixed in him, that Nature might stand up
> And say to all the world, This was a man.)

Earth, Water, Air and Fire are part of ourselves, and we of them. And through them also the stars are linked with our inner being, for each constellated Sign of the Zodiac is specially related to one of the four elements, and each element therefore to three Signs.

A stone falls to the ground—we see it seeking the centre of the earth, moved by something much more like desire than what we to-day call gravity. We prick our finger and a drop of red blood appears. We look at the blood . . . but for the moment I will not pursue this any further. The reader who is at all acquainted with the productions of the medieval mind, its alchemy, its medicine, its herb-lore, its bestiaries, and so forth, can do it better for himself. For the reader who is not so acquainted there are the libraries—

better still, there are those inexhaustible encyclopaedias in stone, the cathedral carvings.

Whatever their religious or philosophical beliefs, men of the same community in the same period share a certain background-picture of the world and their relation to it. In our own age—whether we believe our consciousness to be a soul ensconced in a body, like a ghost in a machine, or some inextricable psychosomatic mixture—when we think *casually*, we think of that consciousness as situated at some point in space, which has no special relation to the universe as a whole, and is certainly nowhere near its centre. Even those who achieve the intellectual contortionism of denying that there is such a thing as consciousness, feel that this denial comes from inside their own skins. Whatever it is that we ought to call our 'selves', our bones carry it about like porters. This was not the background picture before the scientific revolution. The background picture then was of man as a microcosm within the macrocosm. It is clear that he did not feel himself isolated by his skin from the world outside him to quite the same extent as we do. He was integrated or mortised into it, each different part of him being united to a different part of it by some invisible thread. In his relation to his environment, the man of the middle ages was rather less like an island, rather more like an embryo, than we are.

# XII

## SOME CHANGES

In the first chapter of this book it was pointed out that our collective representations compose, not only the world of everyday experience, but also the world which (apart from the special case of physics) is investigated by the sciences. Science did not, of course, begin with the scientific revolution. But in the time before that had done its work, the world with which science had to deal was not that of our own day, but a world of the kind sketched in the last chapter. If, to take only one instance, we look at the theories concerning the blood and its circulation which prevailed before Harvey, we can at once see from their whole character that they represent the application of alpha-thinking to representations quite other than our own. The background-picture of man as microcosm at the centre of the world as macrocosm was more than a background-picture for science. There, and in particular in their chemistry, which we should now call alchemy, that picture became explicit as theory. And where it was not explicit, it was still implied. But it went further than this. Just as for us evolution, for instance, besides being both a background-picture and an explicit theory, has spread itself as a way of thinking, far beyond the confines of biology; or as mechanism has passed from physics into chemistry and physiology; so the medieval background-picture, of a reciprocal participation between man and the elements by which he was surrounded, influenced other sciences besides alchemy. Thus, in medicine, the heart was the central organ, occupying something the same position in the microcosm of man, as did man himself in the macrocosm. It drew the blood into itself, in order to replenish it with *pneuma* or 'vital spirits', after which the blood passed of its own motion back again into the system of the body. Instead of a circulation, there were two different kinds of blood; the arterial, whose function has just been described, and which contained those vital spirits to which we still unknowingly refer when we speak of 'high' or 'low' spirits; and the venous, which flowed back and forth in the veins, conveying nourishment.

We saw in Chapter IV that anthropologists have been particularly struck by the difference between those features which we ourselves select for attention out of the whole representation, and the features which a participating consciousness selects. This seems to be well exemplified in the case of blood, as it appeared and was known before the seventeenth century. The medieval mind was not particularly interested in the mechanical part of the representation; on the other hand, it was much more vividly aware than we are of a qualitative difference between arterial blood and venous blood. Are we sure we are justified in ruling out the possibility that *participated* venous blood and participated arterial blood really are two different kinds of fluid? It is indeed remarkable that earlier still, and down to the time of Galen, it was thought that the arteries did not contain blood at all, but only air.

Harvey, on the other hand, was definitely interested in the *mechanism* of the heart—even to the extent of talking of the heart as 'a piece of machinery in which, though one wheel gives motion to another, yet all the wheels seem to move simultaneously'. This enabled him ultimately to demonstrate the circulation of the blood. And his discovery, like many of the discoveries made in the non-mechanical sciences, had two clearly traceable consequences. On the one hand, it corrected a number of palpable mechanical errors

—for instance, the belief that air passed directly from the lungs to the heart, and that the blood flowed both ways through the veins. On the other hand, it contributed towards the bringing about of an exclusively mechanomorphic view of both blood and heart.

The second consequence took effect only gradually. Harvey himself still assumed the presence of vital spirits and he retained enough participating consciousness to write with enthusiasm on the subject of the heart as the central organ—like a sort of sun—of the human body. The like enthusiasm is observable in Copernicus writing of the 'macrocosmic' sun; and it is clear that a relation between the two was assumed by both men. For Harvey's discovery of the circulation of the blood was based, quite consciously, upon two Aristotelian and medieval doctrines, namely, the participating and formal relation between macrocosm and microcosm to which I have already referred in this chapter, and the 'perfection' of circular motion to which I referred earlier in the book. Thus, the ousting of participation is not a *logical* consequence of a more accurate observation of the mechanical element in any representation; it is a practical one. If we are present at a church service, where a censer is swinging, we may either attend to the whole representation or we may select for attention the actual movement to and fro of the censer. In the latter case, if we are a Galileo,[1] we may discover the law of the pendulum. It is a good thing to discover the law of the pendulum. It is not such a good thing to lose, for that reason, all interest in, and ultimately even perception of, the incense whose savour it was the whole purpose of the pendulum to release. Participation ceases to be conscious precisely because we cease to attend to it. But, as already pointed out, participation does not cease to be a fact because it ceases to be conscious. It merely ceases to be what I have called 'original' participation.

[1] Actually it was not a censer, but a lamp in the Cathedral of Pisa which he was watching.

# Some Changes

From a slightly different point of view, all this could be expressed by saying that words like *blood* and *heart* have shifted their meanings. In maintaining this, I shall of course be accused of confusing the word with the thing. But this is a fallacy. The real confusion lies hidden in the indictment. It is indeed possible, when thinking of the relation between words and things, to forget what 'things', that is phenomena, are; namely, that they are collective representations and, as such, correlative to human consciousness. But those who decline to adopt this expedient, will find it impossible to sever the 'thing' by a sort of surgical operation from its name. The relation between collective representations and language is of the most intimate nature; and if charges of muddled thinking are to be brought, I do not hesitate to say that the boot is on the other leg. Those who insist that words and things are in two mutually exclusive categories of reality are simply confusing the phenomena with the particles. They are trying to think about the former as though they were the latter. Whereas, by definition, it is only the unrepresented which is independent of collective human consciousness and therefore of human language.

The word *blood* is a particularly striking example of such a shift of meaning, since it is a substance with which, as it swings to and fro from heart and lung at the centre to visible complexion and sensitive skin at the periphery, we can still in some measure feel ourselves to be united by an extra-sensory link. We can, for example, both feel within ourselves and see through the curtain of another's flesh how instantly it answers to fear and shame. Thus, we still participate 'originally' in our own blood up to the very moment when it becomes phenomenal by being shed. From that moment on, we abandon it to the mechanomorphism which characterizes all our phenomena. For us—that is, for our casual awareness, though not for our scientific concepts—there are really two kinds of blood: the shed and the unshed; rather as for Galen there were two kinds of blood, the venous and the arterial. Both of Galen's were participated;

whereas only *one* of ours is. We refer to what remains of that participation when we speak, with a psychological intention, of 'bad blood' or 'hot blood'. We no longer distinguish where he did. We do distinguish where he did not, polarizing the old meaning of *blood* into two, a metaphorical and a literal one. And our medicine interests itself almost exclusively in the literal one, that is, in the idol.

# XIII

## THE TEXTURE OF MEDIEVAL THOUGHT

Once the fact of participation is granted, the connection between words and things must, we have seen, be admitted to be at any time a very much closer one than the last two or three centuries have assumed. Conscious participation, moreover, will be aware of that connection; and original participation was conscious. It is only if we approach it in this light that we can hope to understand the extreme preoccupation of medieval learning with words—and with grammar, dialectic, rhetoric, logic and all that has to do with words. For words—and particularly nouns—were not then, and could not then be regarded as *mere* words. I was taught in my first class at school to recite aloud with the rest of the class: 'A noun is the name of anything,' and the philosophers, from Plotinus to Aquinas, were wont to treat at the same time of words and things under the inclusive topic of 'names'. Thus, Dionysius in his *De Divinis Nominibus*, and Aquinas in the 13th Quaestio of Part I of the *Summa* ('concerning the names of God') and in the little treatise *De Natura Verbi Intellectus* and elsewhere, are both concerned, not with philology but with epistemology and metaphysics.

In the last two chapters I have said a little of the world as it was for the common man and a little of the world as it was for science immediately before the scientific revolution. Now I am to say a little of the world as it was shown forth in philosophy. In all cases the plan of this book as well as the time at my disposal both for study and for writing, have determined that that little must be a very little indeed. I am only too well aware that a whole book, instead of a chapter, would not be too much to give to the philosophy alone of that lost world. Once again, it *is* a lost world—although the whole purpose of this book is to show that its spiritual wealth can be, and indeed, if incalculable disaster is to be avoided, *must* be regained. No good can come of any attempt to hark back to the original participation from which it sprang.

That lost world, then, was a world in which both phenomenon and name were felt as representations. On the one hand 'the word conceived in the mind is representative of the whole of that which is realized in thought' (*Verbum igitur in mente conceptum est repraesentativum omnis ejus quod actu intelligitur*).[1] But on the other hand the phenomenon itself only achieves full reality (*actus*) in the moment of being 'named' by man; that is, when that in nature which it represents is united with that in man which the name represents. Such naming, however, need not involve vocal utterance. For the name or word is not mere sound, or mere ink. For Aquinas, as for Augustine, there are, anterior to the uttered word, the intellect-word, the heart-word and the memory-word (*verbum intellectus, verbum cordis, verbum memoriae*). The human word proceeds from the memory, as the Divine Word proceeds from the Father.[2] Proceeds from it, yet remains one with it. For the world is the thought of God realized through His Word. Thus, the Divine Word is also *forma exemplaris*;[3] the phenomena are its representations; as the human word is the representation of *intellectus in actu*. But, once again, the phenomenon itself only achieves its full reality (*actus*) in being named or thought by man; for thinking in act *is* the thing thought, in act; just as the senses in act, are the things sensed, in act. (*Intellectus in*

---

[1] *Summa Theologica*, 1a, Qu. 34, a. 3.
[2] *De Differentia Divini Verbi et Humani; De Natura Verbi Intellectus*, etc.
[3] *Summa*, 1a, Qu. 3, a. 8, ad 2.

*actu est intelligibile in actu; sicut sensus in actu est sensibile in actu.*[1] And elsewhere St. Thomas expressly ratifies the dictum of Aristotle in his *De Anima*, that 'the soul is in a manner all things': (*Anima est quodammodo omnia*).[2]

It is against a background of thoughts like these, and of the collective representations on which they were based, that we must see the medieval conception of the Seven Liberal Arts, with Grammar at their head, followed immediately by Rhetoric and Dialectic. To learn about the true nature of words was at the same time to learn about the true nature of things. And it was the only way. We may reflect how the meaning of the word *grammar* itself has been polarized, since the scientific revolution, into the study of 'mere' words, on the one hand, and, on the other, into the half-magical *gramarye*, which altered its form to *glamour* and was useful for a season to the poets, before it was debased. One may reflect also on the frequent appearances made by Grammar and the other liberal arts, as persons, in medieval allegory, and how easily and naturally they mingle there with the strange figure of the Goddess Natura—at once so like and so unlike the Persephone of Greek mythology. This might easily lead us into a consideration of allegory itself—a literary form which is so little to our taste, and yet was so popular and all-pervasive in the Middle Ages. Is it not clear that *we* find allegory desiccated precisely because, for us, mere words are themselves desiccated—or rather because, for us, words are 'mere'? For us, the characters in an allegory are 'personified abstractions', but for the man of the Middle Ages Grammar or Rhetoric, Mercy or 'Daunger', were real to begin with, simply *because* they were 'names'. And names could be representations, in much the same solid-feeling way as things were.

For this very reason we are in some danger of confusing their allegory with the 'symbolism' in which we ourselves are again beginning to be interested, or at least of judging them by the same standards. This is an error. Symbolism

[1] Ibid., 1a, Qu. 12, a. 2. 3.    [2] Ibid., 1a, Qu. 14, a. 1.

often expresses itself in language, as so much else does, though it can also express itself through other media. Yet the essence of symbolism is, not that words or names, as such, but that things or events themselves, are apprehended as representations. But this, as we have seen, is the normal way of apprehension for a participating consciousness. *Our* 'symbolical' therefore is an approximation to, or a variant of, *their* 'literal'. Even when they got down to the bedrock of literal, they still experienced that rock as a representation. And so Aquinas, in dealing with the use of language in Holy Scripture, first divides its meaning into *literal* and *spiritual* and then subsumes the *allegorical* (and certain other) interpretations under the heading of *spiritual*. But when he comes to the *sensus parabolicus* (which is our 'symbolical') he includes it in the literal (*sub literali continetur*). When, for example, in the Bible, 'the right arm of God' is spoken of, 'It is not the figure, but the figured which is the literal meaning'.[1] All this will bear some meditation.

Indeed, to understand how the word 'literal' has changed its meaning is to understand the heart of the matter. For our problem is, precisely, to transport ourselves into the interior of minds, for which the *ordinary* way of looking at, and of thinking about, phenomena, was to look at and to think about them as appearances—representations. For which, therefore, knowledge was defined, not as the devising of hypotheses, but as an act of union with the represented behind the representation. And it is only by reconstructing in imagination, and not just in theory, the nature of the representations they confronted that we can hope really to understand the mode of their thinking. If we approach it from this end, instead of, as is usual, by way of our own representations and our own consequent distortions of the then meanings of their terms, then the Scholastic terminology does indeed spring into life for us—form and matter, *actus* and *potentia*, species, essence, existence, the active and the passive intelligence, and the rest. We must forget all about

---

[1] *Summa*, 1a, Qu. 1, a. 10, ad 3.

our 'laws of nature', those interposed, spectral hypotheses, before we can understand the 'forms' of medieval scholasticism. For the forms determined the appearances, not as laws do, but rather as a soul determines a body; and indeed the animal and human soul was defined as the 'form' of the body. We must forget all about causality, as we understand it, if we want to understand how the form was also *causa exemplaris*. But there is not anything to forget, for we have not even a transmuted survival, of that *actus*: *potentia* polarity, which was the very life-blood of Scholastic thought, central in its heart and manifest, through its capillaries, at all points of its surface organism. Being is potential existence; existence actualizes being. Yet, in the universe, *actus* precedes *potentia*; for out of potentiality a subject cannot be brought except by a being that is actual. The being of God is wholly actual, and is at the same time His existence; but, for creatures, it is only their *existence* which actualizes—actualizes not their own being, but the being of God, which they participate. Everywhere around us we must see creatures in a state of *potentia* being raised to *actus*: and yet, behind the appearances, the *actus* is already there. What is the intellectual soul but the potentiality of determining the species of things? And what are the phenomena themselves? *Actually* the likenesses or representations of all sorts of 'species'— but *potentially* (that is, in the condition described as *in potentia*) immaterial in the soul itself.[1] Phenomena and mind in perpetual interplay, with 'species' hovering somewhere between them as the moment in which the one becomes the other—*Anima enim quasi transformata est in rem per speciem.*[2]

'Knowledge', for such a consciousness, was conceived of as the perfection or completion of the 'naming' process of thought. In ordinary thinking or speaking, as in perception, the participation was a half-conscious process. But knowledge was an actual union with the represented behind the representation. 'The knowledge of things that are, *is* the

---

[1] Ibid., 1a, Qu. 79, a 4, ad 4.
[2] Aquinas, *De Natura Verbi Intellectus*.

things', (*Cognitio eorum, quae sunt, ea, quae sunt, est*) wrote John Scotus Erigena in the seventh century, quoting Dionysius. 'Nothing', wrote Aquinas, 'is known except truth—which is the same as being.' (*nihil enim scitur nisi verum, quod cum ente convertitur*)[1] Or, as a mean between *potentia* and *actus*, it was the process of actualization of the soul's potentiality to become what it contemplated, and thus, a stage on its journey back to God. God's own knowledge was alike the cause of all things and identical with His substance, and man participated in the being of God. Indeed, it was only by virtue of that participation that he could claim to *have* any being.

Now, participation, as an actual *experience*, is only to be won for our islanded consciousness of to-day by special exertion. It is a matter, not of theorizing, but of 'imagination' in the genial or creative sense of the word, and therefore our first glimpse of it is commonly an aesthetic experience of some sort, derived from poetry or painting. And yet this experience, so foreign to our habit, is one which we positively must acquire and apply before we can hope to understand the thought of any philosopher earlier than the scientific revolution. Without it we shall not really understand what they mean when they use the commonest terms —species and genus, form and matter, subject and accident, cause and effect. Instead, we shall clumsily substitute a meaning of our own. In the work of Thomas Aquinas, in particular, the word *participate* or *participation* occurs almost on every page, and a whole book could be written—indeed one has been written[2]—on the uses he makes of it. It is not a technical term of philosophy and he is no more concerned to define it than a modern philosopher would be, to define some such common tool of his thought as, say, the word *compare*. Only in one passage, from the whole of his voluminous works, according to M. Geiger, did he feel it neces-

[1] *Summa*, 1a, Qu. 1, a 1, 2.
[2] L.–B. Geiger, *La Participation dans la Philosophie de S. Thomas d'Aquin.* Paris, 1942.

sary to indicate its meaning, and this he did principally by illustrating it. Thus, after telling us that the species participates the genus, and the subject the accident, that matter participates form and effect participates cause, he gives us a glimpse of what all these participations signify to him, by adding: 'Suppose we say that air participates the light of the sun, because it does not receive it in that clarity in which it is in the sun.'[1]

At one end of the scale the subject participates its predicate[2]; at the other end, a formal or hierarchical participation *per similitudinem* was the foundation of the whole structure of the universe; for all creatures were in a greater or lesser degree images or representations, or 'names' of God, and their likeness or unlikeness did not merely measure, but *was* the nearer or more distant emanation of His Being and Goodness in them. It was a spiritual structure, and much of it lay beyond the world of appearance altogether. Angels, for example, are not simply the subject of a separate work, or a separate chapter of the *Summa*, but occur everywhere in it and are as likely to be referred to in a purely epistemological, as in a cosmological, context.

It will be well to point out here that, if I have concentrated on one particular medieval philosopher, rather than attempted a conspectus of the whole field of medieval philosophy or theories of knowledge, it is because that is the method which a history of consciousness, as distinct from a history of ideas, must adopt. It must attempt to penetrate into the very texture and activity of thought, rather than to collate conclusions. It is concerned, semantically, with the way in which words are used rather than with the product of discourse. Expressed in terms of logic, its business is more with the proposition than with the syllogism and more with the term than with the proposition. Therefore it must particularize. It must choose some one, or at best a few points, for its penetration. It is a question of making the best choice, and to me the best choice seemed to be the language

---

[1] *De Hebdomadibus*, cap. 2.    [2] Cf. p. 31.

and thought of Thomas Aquinas. I could probably have found more sensational illustrations of participation in, for example, Erigena or Albertus. For the Arabians, participation—with a particular intellectual emphasis—was so complete as practically to exclude individual human identity. I should, I think, have found fewer illustrations among the Nominalists, but they can fairly be regarded as forerunners of the scientific revolution, in whom the decline of participation cast its shadow before. Moreover, in the mind of Aquinas, with his enormous erudition, the whole corpus of medieval thought is in a manner recapitulated; and he is as sober as he is profound.

# XIV

# BEFORE AND AFTER THE SCIENTIFIC REVOLUTION

For medieval man, then, the universe was a kind of theophany, in which he participated at different levels, in being, in thinking, in speaking or naming, and in knowing. And then—the evolutionary change began. Not, of course, at any given moment, but with anticipations, localized delays, individual differences. But no beginning is instantaneous—otherwise the very word 'begin' would be unnecessary and indeed meaningless. We need not pay too much attention to those historians who cautiously refuse to detect any process in history, because it is difficult to divide into periods, or because the periods are difficult to date precisely. The same objections apply to the process of growth from child to man. We should rather remind them that, if there is no process, there is in fact no such thing as history at all, so that they themselves must be regarded as mere chroniclers and antiquarians—a limitation which I cannot fancy they would relish. Moreover, the mental image, which they transfer to history, of a formless process determined by the chance impact of events, is itself, as we saw in Chapter IX, a product of the idolatry of the age of literalness.

However this may be, and whatever chronological limits we choose to assign to it, a change there certainly was. Professor Butterfield has commented well on it:

> through changes in the habitual use of words, certain things in the natural philosophy of Aristotle had now

acquired a coarsened meaning or were actually misunder-
stood. It may not be easy to say why such a thing should
have happened, but men unconsciously betray the fact
that a certain Aristotelian thesis simply has no meaning
for them any longer—they just cannot think of the stars
and heavenly bodies as things without weight even when
the books tells them to do so. Francis Bacon seems unable
to say anything except that it is obvious that these
heavenly bodies have weight, like any other kind of
matter which we meet in our experience. Bacon says,
furthermore, that he is unable to imagine the planets as
nailed to crystalline spheres; and the whole idea only
seems more absurd to him if the spheres in question are
supposed to be made of that liquid, aethereal kind of substance which Aristotle had in mind. Between the idea of
a stone aspiring to reach its natural place at the centre of
the universe—and rushing more fervently as it came
nearer home—and the idea of a stone accelerating its
descent under the constant force of gravity, there is an
intellectual transition which involves a change in men's
feeling for matter.[1]

We have seen that this change in men's feeling for matter
is merely one aspect of a much deeper and more fundamental change. And the change in men's feeling for the
nature of words and of thought was no whit less marked.
Thus, the polarity of *actus* and *potentia* had carried perhaps
half the weight of the philosophical thought of the Western
mind through all the centuries that elapsed between Aristotle and Aquinas. A medieval philosopher would not have
put the argument as I was obliged to do, when I said in
Chapter III that there is 'no such thing' as unfelt solidity,
just as there is no such thing as an unseen rainbow. He
would have said that both the unseen rainbow and the unfelt matter are *in potentia*. Yet this polarity, taken for granted
for more than a thousand years by some of the acutest

[1] *Origins of Modern Science*, p. 104.

intellects the world has ever known—this polarity has become, for Bacon, a 'frigida distinctio'—mere words! Again, in the *Novum Organum* he tells men bluntly that they ought not to think of 'forms' any more. They are really more like 'laws'.

It may be that nothing really exists except individual bodies, which produce real motion according to law; in science it is just that law, and the inquiry, discovery and explanation of it, which are the fundamental requisite both for the knowledge and for the control of Nature. And it is that law and its 'clauses', which *I* mean when I use (chiefly because of its current prevalence and familiarity) the word 'forms'.[1]

*Causa exemplaris* is gone, in other words, and mechanical causality and the idols are already in sight.

If, with the help of some time-machine working in reverse, a man of the Middle Ages could be suddenly transported into the skin of a man of the twentieth century, seeing through our eyes and with our 'figuration' the objects we see, I think he would feel like a child who looks for the first time at a photograph through the ingenious magic of a stereoscope. 'Oh!' he would say, 'look how they *stand out!*' We must not forget that in his time perspective had not yet been discovered, nor underrate the significance of this. True, it is no more than a device for pictorially representing depth, and separateness, in space. But how comes it that the device had never been discovered before—or, if discovered, never adopted? There were plenty of skilled artists, and they would certainly have hit upon it soon enough if depth in space had characterized the collective representations they wish to reproduce, as it characterizes ours. They did not need it. Before the scientific revolution the world was more like a garment men wore about them than a stage on which they moved. In such a world the convention of perspective was unnecessary. To such a world other conventions of

[1] *Novum Organum*, II, 2. Author's translation.

visual reproduction, such as the nimbus and the halo, were as appropriate as to ours 'they are not. It was as if the observers were themselves *in* the picture. Compared with us, they felt themselves and the objects around them and the words that expressed those objects, immersed together in something like a clear lake of—what shall we say?—of 'meaning', if you choose. It seems the most adequate word. Aquinas's *verbum intellectus* was *tanquam speculum, in quo res cernitur*[1]—'like a mirror in which the object is discerned'.

It happened that, at a time when I was studying the *De Natura Verbi Intellectus*, with that peculiar mixture of perplexity and delight which Thomas's sentences arouse, when his thinking is at its intensest and tersest, I had the good fortune to receive from a friend the gift of a volume of his own poems. It seemed to me then, and it still seems to me now, that in one of them he has managed, without setting out to do so, to convey more vividly than I could ever hope to do, the qualitative difference between a participating outlook on the world, and our own. I therefore conclude my chapter with it.

## REFLECTION

*When hill, tree, cloud, those shadowy forms*
*Ascending heaven are seen,*
*Their mindless beauty I from far*
*Admire, a gulf between;*


*Yet in the untroubled river when*
*Their true ideas I find,*
*That river, joined in trance with me,*
*Becomes my second mind.*[2]

[1] *De Natura Verbi Intellectus.*
[2] George Rostrevor Hamilton. *The Carved Stone.* Heinemann. 1952.

## XV

## THE GRAECO-ROMAN AGE
## (MIND AND MOTION)

Earlier in this book, and particularly in Chapter X, attention was drawn to the difference between a history of thought or of ideas, on the one hand, and a history of consciousness on the other. I am of course aware that the various expressions of medieval thought which I have discussed in the last two chapters are usually explained in quite a different way. Where I have treated them as arising out of, and betokening, a slightly different relation between the mind of man and his phenomena—and that itself as implying slightly different phenomena—the ordinary view regards them purely and simply as a different ideology superimposed on phenomena which were in all respects the same as our own. By tracing this ideology through a chain of individual thinkers—Plato, Aristotle, the Neo-Platonists, Galen, Isidore of Seville, Vincent de Beauvais, Martianus Capella and others—the medieval outlook is presented as a stage in the history of (largely erroneous) ideas.

Now one outstanding thinker does, of course, pass on his ideas to others, and especially so in an age when books are few and hard to come by. There is, therefore, also a valid and significant history of ideas as such. But the irreconcilable conflict between the two approaches—if what we are seeking is a fundamentally *adequate* history of the human mind—becomes especially apparent when we look back, as I endeavoured to do in the last chapter, on the ideas which the Western mind has formed in the past about this very question, of its own relation to the phenomena, or in other words, when we survey its theories of knowledge. We must, then, make our choice. The whole basis of epistemology from Aristotle to Aquinas assumed participation, and the problem was merely the precise manner in which that participation operated. We can either conclude that this persistent assumption was a piece of elaborate self-deception, which just happened to last, not only from Aristotle but from the beginnings of human thought down to the fifteenth or sixteenth century A.D., or we can assume that there really was participation. I should find the second hypothesis the less fantastic of the two, even if it were not necessary, on other and quite unhistorical grounds (as I have suggested that it is), to accept participation as the permanent ground of our collective representations.

It is to me rather too flattering a view to take of the philosophers, not excepting even Aristotle, to regard them as the efficient and sufficient causes of collective representations shared by the greater part of Western Humanity for nearly twenty centuries. From the point of view of a history of consciousness, their writings are rather landmarks to indicate the nature of that consciousness, inasmuch as they represent the human mind in its most wakeful state. At the same time, owing to the subtle link between thinking and figuration, and to the part played by language in evoking and sustaining the collective representations, they are by no means without causal significance. On either view, whether we choose to treat the history of the mind as a history of ideology or as a history of consciousness, we shall find that the continuity between Greek and medieval epistemology is far more striking than the break; and again, on either view, the language and the thought of Plato and Aristotle are the twin strands about which that continuity clusters.

For the history of the mind—above all, when it is treated as a history of consciousness—the periods into which it is most convenient and most significant to divide the past history of mankind, will not be those familiar ones which are adapted to a more superficial record. From the former point of view, the Graeco-Roman period is seen as extending, practically unbroken, to the end of the Middle Ages. And beyond it; for the scientific revolution took some three or four centuries to accomplish completely, and participation died not suddenly but by inches. It survived, for example, in chemistry longer than in the other sciences and, after it had vanished altogether, not only from the sciences but from the collective representations of the educated, or at least the urbanized part of mankind, its echo continued to survive in their habitual use of language for the purposes of thought. It is indeed only in our own time that we are witnessing its eviction from that final stronghold.

We have already seen that logical predication was based by Aquinas on participation. Is it not apparent to reflection, that the validity of alpha-thinking, in so far as it is based on logic, rests on that very participation which it tends, by its operation, to destroy? We can continue to apprehend phenomena as participating one another, in a way which renders logical predication meaningful, only as long as we continue to apprehend them as participated by ourselves. When that ceases, they become idols, and idols do not participate one another. Nor are they connected in any necessary way with their *names*. They are simply 'there'. Accordingly, the names cannot meaningfully be predicated of each other. In the logic of, for instance, John Stuart Mill, a certain residue of participation is still tacitly assumed. Where that has finally vanished and idolatry is total, *species*, *genus* and the rest of them vanish, as realities. Thus, early in the twentieth century, formal logic begins to boggle much more heavily at the notion of predication, and really to *feel* the difficulty of distinguishing it from an assertion of numerical identity. Sooner or later a Wittgenstein or an Ayer inevitably arises, convinced that all predication must be either false or tautologous—a state of mind which was playfully foreshadowed by Plato more than two thousand years ago in his dialogue, *The Sophist*. To this point of view, the belief that in the act of predication the mind is operating, not only on words but on things themselves, can only appear as a kind of survival of totemism. And that is indeed what it is, if for 'totemism' we substitute 'participation'.[1]

The aim of the three preceding chapters was, to characterize the collective representations of the period immediately preceding the scientific revolution, in the particular respect in which they differed most from our own. They were mainly illustrated from the close of that period in what are called the Middle Ages; but most of what was said applies with equal or greater force to the Graeco-Roman age proper, in which the period began. As far as participation is concerned, the difference between medieval and Greek thought is one of degree rather than of kind; and I shall limit myself to a very few observations on the latter. In the first place, there are strong indications in the Greek language and elsewhere, apart altogether from philosophy, that the participation of the ordinary man was a livelier and more immediate experience. The gods and nature-spirits of Greek mythology, and, in particular, the whole Dionysian element in the cults, linked man and nature in a unity which for a very good reason could not, as we shall see, and did not survive the impact of Christianity. But apart from religion, if we are attentive to the *nuances* of the Greek language, we shall find many signs of a living participation in nature—especially perhaps the nature of man's own bodily processes—of which we to-day know next to no-

---

[1] Cf. pp. 31 and 90. Very shortly, the difficulty about predication out of which logical positivism etc. arose is the following: If I say *a horse is an animal*, then (*a*) if by the word *animal* I mean something more, or less, or other than *horse*, I have told a lie; but (*b*) if I do *not* mean by the word *animal* something more, or less, or other than *horse*, I have said almost nothing. For I might as well have said *a horse is a horse*. Hence the attempts we are now witnessing to replace the traditional logic based on predication by a new logic, in which symbols of algebraic precision refer to 'atomic' facts and events having no vestige of connection with the symbols and no hierarchical relation to each other.

thing. I feel, moreover, that the superlative quality of Greek sculpture at its height must be attributed to that participation, rather than to any mere excellence in the craft of meticulous imitation.

At the philosophical level, we may reflect from this point of view on the very title of that work of Aristotle from which Aquinas quotes more freely than from any other. In English it is *On the Soul*; in Latin *De Anima*; but in Greek it is Περὶ ψυχῆς, and ψυχή (*psyche*) was in Greek the word for 'life' as well as for 'soul'. Again, there is a sinewy quality in Aristotle's νοῦς ποιητικός and νοῦς παθητικός (*nous poieticus* and *nous patheticus*), which has already faded somewhat from their Latin equivalents *intellectus agens* and *intellectus possibilis*. The *nous* of which Aristotle spoke and thought was clearly less subjective than Aquinas's *intellectus*; and when he deals with the problem of perception, he polarizes not merely the mind, but the world itself, without explanation or apology, into the two *verbs* ποιεῖν and πάσχειν (*poiein* and *paschein*) ('to do' and 'to suffer'). In the psychological and epistemological contexts in which he employs them, these two words alone are as untranslatable as the mentality which they reveal is remote from our own. It is, for instance, not possible to equate them with the Aristotelian 'matter' and 'form', though matter is certainly passive and form active. For, in the process of perception (he tells us) it is the percept which is active and the perceiving organism which is passive. The organ of perception *is* potentially what the percept already is actually; it 'suffers' something unlike itself, but in doing so becomes like what it suffers. The actualization (ἐνέργεια) of percept and of perception are one and the same thing. When we come to thinking, on the other hand, as distinct from perceiving, while it is the passive mind (*nous patheticus*) which gives us our subjectivity, it is the active mind (*nous poieticus*) which is operative in the act of knowing. The soul is *poiein* to the body's *paschein*; but soul and body together are (except in the act of knowing) *nous patheticus*. Alike in perceiving and in thinking, there is an active and a passive *movement*, and in both cases the second is the field for the activity of the first. All these complex movements, which are the very stuff of human nature, may be conceived of as potential knowledge; actual knowledge occurs when man becomes wakefully aware of them; for then (νοῦς γίγνεται ἕκαστα[1] . . . τὸ δ'αὐτό ἐστιν ἡ κατ' ἐνέργειαν ἐπιστήμη τῷ πράγματι)[2] mind becomes what it thinks and may be said to know itself.

If this kind of psychology was really as tenuous, fine-drawn and obscure—or, to use Bacon's word, as 'frigid'—as it seems to most people to-day, it is difficult to explain why, for so many centuries, so many people found it exciting. The true explanation is, once more, that we have lost half the meanings of the key-words in which it is expressed. Above all, with the disappearance of participation, words to do with thinking and perceiving and words to do with movement and space have parted company. Aristotle's *poiein* and *paschein* were for him, not the insubstantial, semi-mystical abstractions which we make of them, when we translate them '*active principle*' and '*passive principle*'. They were, at the same time, respectively, κινεῖν and κινεῖσθαι—'To-move', and 'To-be-moved'. Locomotion or traction was for the Greek philosophers only one kind of movement, which included also, change, growth and decay; and the *kinesis*, to which Aristotle refers in so many different contexts, was simply not what we mean by 'movement' at all, who think of it as the bare change of position of an idol in Newtonian space.

If we would gain some idea, not only of what 'movement' meant before the scientific revolution, but also of that, to us, either foolish or baffling tendency to connect pure thought somehow with space, which we have already observed in the case of Plato's astronomy, we shall find it more pronounced and explicit in the thought of Plato and his predecessors than in that of Aristotle and his successors. In

---

[1] Aristotle, *De Anima*, Bk. III, Ch. iv.
[2] Ibid., Bk. III, Ch. vii.

the *Theaetetus*, for instance, Plato tells us that for Heraclitus and his followers *poiein* and *paschein* (let me now call them *action* and *passion*) were the two primary kinds of *kinesis*, and that it is out of them that sense-perception arises. Each of the two was again subdivided into swift and slow. What we call 'the object' was slow *action* and what we call the 'subject' slow *passion*; while what we call the 'quality' of the object was swift *action*, and what we call 'sensation', swift *passion*. It is with such images in our minds that we should read Plato himself, when he maintains elsewhere that through perception we share or participate (κοινωνεῖν) in the process of coming into being (γένεσις). It is with such images in our minds that we should seek to interpret, if we really wish to enter it, the thought of Aristotle and the philosophy and science of the Middle Ages in which so much of that thought lived on.

As to the relation between thought and space, it is almost sufficient to read the *Timaeus*—which, incidentally, was the principal channel through which the thinking of Plato and his predecessors was known to the Middle Ages. In this dialogue, Plato describes the world as 'a moving image of eternity'. It is however not simply a matter of a few revealing uses of key-words, though of these there are enough and to spare: as when he tells us that of the seven different kinds of movement, movement in a circle is ἡ περὶ νοῦν καὶ φρόνησιν μάλιστα οὖσα—'the one that has most to do with mind and understanding', or again, that by contemplating the undisturbed revolutions (περίοδοι) of mind in the heavens we may make use of them for the revolutions of our own intellect, which, though disturbed, are nevertheless akin to the former. It is rather that the whole development and structure of thought in the dialogue is such that celestial astronomy and metaphysics are inextricably one. In the metaphysical discussion of the problem of the one and the many, of identity and difference (which Plato here names *same* and *other*), the abstract notion of sameness is indistinguishable from 'the Circle of the Same' (namely the cele-

stial equator), and the abstract notion of difference is indistinguishable from 'the Circle of the Other' (namely the
Ecliptic, where the planets wander and change).

We have already seen that even in the Middle Ages man's
experience of space was clearly different from our own, and
the old tendency to experience as one what we now distinguish absolutely as 'mind', on the one hand, and 'space' on
the other, still finds an echo in the *Divine Comedy*, especially
when in the 10th Canto of the *Paradiso* Dante refers to the
celestial revolutions as:

> Quanto per mente o per loco si gira.[1]

The impression we get, however, is that it was by then already a good deal nearer to our own than the Greek experience. It is interesting in this connection to observe how
Aristotle selects for criticism precisely that astronomical
metaphysics to which I have just referred, maintaining that
the oneness, or self-identity of *nous* ought not to be conceived spatially (κατὰ τὸ μέγεθος) but only numerically,
and that accordingly the Circles of which Plato speaks in the
*Timaeus* must be ruled out when we are treating of psychology. The proper movement of a circle is revolution; but
the proper movement of mind, he insists, is—thinking.
This detachment of the idea of thought, first from the idea
of movement in space, and then from the idea of movement
of any sort, must have been no small feat. It was the beginning of true beta-thinking.

Here we may well pause for a moment to refer back to
Harvey's discovery of the circulation of the blood. It will be
remembered from Chapter XII that this was based on the
perfection of circular motion and on the formal relation
between microcosm and macrocosm. Here then is a striking
example of the diminishing experience of participation. First
the great circles of the macrocosm are abstracted by Aristotle from the movement of mind and conceived as more
purely spatial, and then, much later, this very abstraction

[1] Whatsoever revolves through mind or space.

facilitates a mechanomorphic conception of the movement of the blood. Later still, this conception of the blood plays its part in obliterating from consciousness the whole relation of microcosm to macrocosm on which it was based.

Although Aristotle was the pupil of Plato, there are many good reasons for treating the former as beginning a new epoch, and the latter as closing an old one, while not forgetting that all such exact limitations of period have about them something artificial and arbitrary. At some point a thing ceases to be flower and becomes fruit; but who shall say exactly when? In Raphael's fresco of the *School of Athens* in the Vatican, the two figures of Plato and Aristotle stand side by side, the one with raised hand pointing upwards to the heavens, the other pointing earthward down a flight of steps. If, in imagination, we take our stand between the two, we can indeed look forward, through the thinking which found expression in Aristotle, to the collective representations of the Western world which were to take their course, through the so-called dark and middle ages, down to the scientific revolution and beyond. While through the other, through the star-and-space-involved thinking of Plato, we may peer backward into the collective representations of the East and of the past. The cosmogony of Plato was still in the Pythagorean stream, and the tradition that Pythagoras visited India, whether in itself it be legendary or historical, is a convenient expression of a process which is apparent from internal evidence. It is many years now since Max Müller pointed to a number of coincidences between the philosophy of Plato and the Upanishads, among them the concept of reincarnation, but added that he thought any actual contact unlikely. But if what has been said in this book (particularly Chapter X) is correct, the progress of ideas has been as much, or more, a function of the evolution of consciousness than its vehicle. That is, of consciousness and its correlative, the phenomena or collective representations. Accordingly, that evolution is much less dependent on contacts or communications than has generally been supposed.

When we consider, as is here being attempted, the evolution of consciousness as the progressive decline of participation, the emergence of the Greek from the ancient oriental outlook is a fact which we can contemplate without being unduly troubled by the absence of biographical details about Pythagoras. Anyone who has struggled for a few pages with the Vedas in translation, will know that in their language the entanglement of subject and object, of psychology and natural history, of divine and human, of word and thing, is such as to render the thought virtually unintelligible to a modern reader—though of course he can make some kind of 'sense' of it by paraphrasing it into moralizing abstractions of his own. To take only one instance, the word *Namarupa*, or 'name-form', takes us back straight away to a stage of consciousness at which that surgical operation, to which I referred in Chapter XII, whereby the thing is separated from its name, had not yet begun to be performed. In the measure that man participates his phenomena, in that measure the name *is* the form, and the form is the name.

At this point, however—that is, with the emergence of Greek thought, so far as it was Platonically inclined, from the hitherto almost wholly religious consciousness of the Orient—I propose to end the movement of this book in the direction of the past and turn its face once more toward the present. To do otherwise would, in the first place, require an acquaintance with oriental languages which I do not possess. But there is another reason. The kind of consciousness which I have hitherto attempted to depict, though characterized by a participation which we lack, is at least, as it were, within sight of our own. We can—or so I have thought—catch glimpses of it which are describable, though with difficulty, in the idol-infected language which the scientific revolution has bequeathed to us. But to depict the kind of consciousness which prevailed at still earlier periods requires, it seems to me, a different method and a different terminology. It may well also demand the extension of historical imagination into a manner of clairvoyance. My purpose is the humbler one of establishing, in the language and imagery of everyday, the bare fact that there has been an evolution of consciousness; and if that is possible at all, it is possible within the limits of Pythagoras and Moses.

# XVI

## ISRAEL

We have been tracing the gradual disappearance of participation; and hitherto, save for a passing reference in Chapter. X, we have considered it only in relation to the growth of that alpha-thinking which first began to play a predominant part in human consciousness with the emergence of Greek civilization from the Orient. But while this was going on, there was another force, quite independent of it, at work in quite a different way to produce the same result. This was the religious impulse of the Jewish nation. And although the two impulses operated to produce the same result, there could hardly be a greater contrast than that which we find between them.

Turn from an Attic chorus or a Platonic dialogue to, say, the 104th Psalm and you are at once in a different climate of soul altogether. More than that, you are among different representations.

*Thou deckest thyself with light as it were with a garment; and spreadest out the heavens like a curtain,* we read in verse two, and for a moment we are inclined to feel that the Psalmist, too, is experiencing the representations as representations, and the world as a theophany. But as we read on, we are impressed more and more with the enormous difference between this world and the world either of Greek or of medieval man. If we seek a parallel in Western literature, we shall almost find it more readily in a later age when participation had nearly vanished—Traherne perhaps, or even Walt Whitman. For here is not only no hint of mythology, but no real suggestion of manifestation. Everything proclaims the glory of God, but nothing represents Him. Nothing could be more beautiful, and nothing could be less Platonic.

*The high hills are a refuge for the wild goats; and so are the stony rocks for the conies*, but it is not, we are made to feel, by contemplating these phenomena that we shall rise to the contemplation of the invisible Divinity who brought them into being. Here, too, the appearances are indeed grounded in divinity; but they are not grounded in the same way. They are not appearances—still less, 'names'—*of* God. They are things created *by* God. There is, in short, nothing to suggest 'immanence', and everything to suggest the contrary.

If, moreover, we review the Old Testament as a whole, we shall scarcely find there suggested what we find *assumed* by both Aristotle and Aquinas, namely, that knowledge of God's creation can become knowledge of God. In the Old Testament the relation of man to God is the only thing that is of any importance at all, but it has nothing to do with detailed knowledge—unless by that we mean a knowledge of the moral law. Of knowledge, as conscious participation in the divine ground of nature, and thus in the Spirit of God Himself, we hear no whisper. The Jew could rejoice in the appearances; but he was not curious about them. He was not *interested* in them. He was, above all, detached from them.

We have seen that, before the days of 'hypotheses to save the appearances', knowledge was inconceivable except as a form of participation, and we cannot resist the conclusion that this detachment from knowledge arose, in the case of the Jews, not so much from any want of mental alertness as from a positive objection to participation as such. We cannot resist this conclusion because the whole history of the race, from Exodus onwards, is the story of that chronic objection.

Participation and the experience of phenomena as representations go hand in hand; and the experience of representations, as such, is closely linked with the making of images. The children of Israel became a nation and began their history in the moment when Moses, in the very heart of the ancient Egyptian civilization, delivered to them those ten commandments, which include the unheard-of injunction: 'Thou shalt not make unto thee any graven image or any likeness of anything that is in heaven above, or that is in the earth beneath, or that is in the water under the earth.' This is perhaps the *unlikeliest* thing that ever happened. As far as we know, in every other nation at that time there prevailed unquestioned the participating consciousness which apprehends the phenomena as representations and naturally expresses itself in making images. For the Jews, henceforward, any dealings with those nations were strictly forbidden. Everywhere throughout the world original participation was in full swing. For the Jews, from that moment on, original participation, and anything smacking of it, became a deadly sin. And what is the Old Testament but the tale of their long struggle against that very sin, their repeated relapses and their final victory?

By the Jewish nation participation was even apprehended as a kind of incontinence; and it often involved incontinence in the narrower sense. Call before your mind the picture of Phinehas in Shittim, seizing a javelin in his right hand and staying the general relapse into idolatry by transfixing his compatriot in the very arms of the Midianitish woman— and you have a device which will serve well enough for Israel's escutcheon; as Pallas Athene, new-born fully armed, from the *brain* of Zeus, will serve as a device for the Greeks. To be *intensely aware* of participation is, for man, to feel the centre of energy in himself identified with the energy of which external nature is the image. Thus, in the religious aspect, original participation has always tended to express itself in cults of a phallic nature. The proper role played by the phallic emblem, as image of man's participation in a

Nature apprehended (as later also in myth and poetry) as female, may be easily conceived. The degeneration of such cults into orgiastic rites and excesses is equally easy—or, for those with no understanding of participation, much easier —to imagine.

The brute acceptance of phenomena at their face value, which was contemned by Plato, is paralleled, in the sphere of the will, by the sensuality which seeks repose or self-extinction in the contacts of the senses, taken as ends in themselves. Both are the passive 'expense' of spirit, replacing its active manifestation. Moreover, participating cults naturally cluster about man-made images; artificial representations evoke and focus the experience of nature as representation; the grove is rendered more numinous by the idol in the grove. Thus the ritual avowal of participation was closely associated with the worship of idols, and the second commandment, already quoted, concludes with the injunction: 'Thou shalt not bow down thyself to them, nor serve them.' Indeed the Jews were not only forbidden to make images; they were not only forbidden to adore or to serve them; they were enjoined to destroy them: 'Ye shall destroy their altars, break their images and cut down their groves.'

Now in this book I have consistently applied the term *idol* to the collective representations characteristic of to-day; I have even defined it, for my purposes, as 'a representation or image which is not experienced as such'. But the heathen idols which the Jews reprobated *were* experienced as such; they *were* participated. It may be felt, therefore, that the term was ill-chosen. The answer to this objection really lies in the book itself, taken as a whole—indeed it *is* the book; but the following observations may not be out of place here.

In a wider frame of reference than that hitherto adopted, *idolatry* may be defined as the valuing of images or representations in the wrong way and for the wrong reasons; and an *idol*, as an image so valued. More particularly, idolatry is the effective tendency to abstract the sense-content from the whole representation and seek that for its own sake, transmuting the admired image into a desired object. This tendency seems always to have been latent in original participation and, if we could peer deep enough into the foundations of the world, we might find it written there that alpha-thinking itself is one of the forms it takes—perhaps the noblest, certainly the subtlest and most lasting form. At all events, the word *idol* has long come to denote, not the image as such (as the Greek *eidolon* originally did), but the image on its way to becoming an object. It does not, therefore, seem to me to be stretching its meaning unduly to extend it to images which have finished that journey.

Striking, as the Jews did, not only at the practice of idolatry, but at the whole religion of the Gentiles centred round it, their impulse was to destroy, not merely that which participation may become, but participation itself. Original participation is, as pointed out in Chapter VI, the sense that their stands behind the phenomena, *and on the other side of them from man*, a represented, which is of the same nature as man. It was against this that Israel's face was set. The devotee in the presence of the totem feels himself and the totem to be filled with the same 'mana'. They are, both of them, 'stopping-places for mana'. It was this state of affairs which Israel consciously arose to destroy. The idols, their Psalmist insisted, were not filled with anything. They were mere hollow pretences of life. They had no 'within'.

> *Their idols are silver and gold: even the work of men's hands.*
> *They have mouths, and speak not: eyes have they, and see not.*
> *They have ears, and hear not: noses have they, and smell not.*
> *They have hands, and handle not: feet have they, and walk not: neither speak they through their throat.*

And, as to their representing anything of the same nature as man, he added ominously:

# Israel

*They that make them are like unto them: and so are all such as put their trust in them.*[1]

There is, accordingly, the deepest imaginable contrast between the non-participation achieved by the children of Israel under the leadership of Moses, and the non-participation achieved by the pagan and Christian West under the influence of Aristotle, though the former accrued in the course of time to the latter. We will here consider three special differences. In the first place, there were no geometrical or mechanical hypotheses to render the appearances 'idols' in the sense in which the word is used in this book. If the children of Israel were enjoined not to worship 'the sun or the moon or any other star', it was because they were *tempted* by the glory of these appearances to do that very thing. They refrained because they were commanded to refrain, not because they had been educated to see the greater light and the less as a ball of gas and a ball of rock, which just happened to be there. It was not, in other words, a *materialist* non-participation. Secondly, their collective representations were necessarily involved with and coloured by their language, and the Ancient Hebrew tongue has a *vocally* representational quality which far exceeds that of any European language living or dead. I shall return to this aspect in a subsequent chapter.

The third difference cannot be displayed in quite such a summary fashion. According to the Old Testament, shortly before the Israelites took their departure from Egypt, the name of the God of Israel was for the first time revealed to them through their representative Moses. And about this Name two things are to be particularly noted. It was regarded as, for the most part, too holy to be communicable. Thus, although in the Psalms, for instance, it will be found *written*, where the word 'Lord' or 'God' is written in the Authorized Version, yet, when it was read aloud, other names such as 'Adonai' (*Lord*) or 'Elohim' were (at all events

[1] Ps. cxv.

by the third century B.C.) vocally substituted. The Name itself was pronounced only by the priests in the Temple when blessing the people or by the High Priest on the Day of Atonement. Other precautions and uses emphasized and preserved its ineffable quality.

Typographically, the Name is represented by four Hebrew consonants. Etymologically, it represents a slight modification of the Hebrew verb 'to be', which also signified 'to breathe'. In Exodus iii, 14—the first revelation—the first person singular of this verb (YHYH) occurs twice, as a verb ('I AM THAT I AM') and once as a noun ('Thus shalt thou say unto the children of Israel, I AM hath sent me unto you.'). In the following verse the third person, YHWH (perhaps the nearest equivalent in English sounds of the so-called 'Tetragrammaton'),[1] is substituted:

> And God said moreover unto Moses, Thus shalt thou say unto the children of Israel: יהוה God of your fathers, the God of Abraham, the God of Isaac, and the God of Jacob, hath sent me unto you: this is my name for ever, and this is my memorial unto all generations.

The Hebrew word for 'Jew' is derived from the same verb; so that a devout Jew could not name his race without recalling, nor affirm his own existence without tending to utter, the Tetragrammaton. Written, as all Hebrew words were, without vowels, when any true child of Israel perused the unspoken Name, יהוה must have seemed to come whispering up, as it were, from the depths of his own being!

That this, or something like it, was increasingly the case is at least suggested by the 'progress' we note between the account in Exodus iii of the experience of Moses and that given in I Kings xix of the experience of Elijah on the occasions of their encounters with God. The Angel of the Lord appeared to Moses in a flame of fire and out of the midst of

---

[1] 'Y' is here consonantal. The vowels in the traditional English form *Jehovah* arise from the custom of inserting between the consonants of the Tetragrammaton the vowels appropriate to the words *Elohim* and *Adonai*.

a bush, and then the Lord Himself called to Moses out of the midst of the same bush. But by the time of Elijah the withdrawal of Israel from participation was already far advanced, and we are given, instead, in the well-known verses, a crescendo of appearances, in each of which God was *not*.

> And, behold, יהוה passed by, and a great and strong wind rent the mountains, and brake in pieces the rocks before יהוה; but יהוה was not in the wind: and after the wind an earthquake; but יהוה was not in the earthquake:
>
> And after the earthquake a fire, but יהוה was not in the fire: and after the fire a still small voice . . .

This ingathering withdrawal from participation, to which the Old Testament points, was clearly, then, a very different matter from that ousting or suppression of participation which alpha-thinking has subsequently accomplished in the Western world. Indeed, it might with equal truth be described as a concentration or centripetal *deepening* of participation. As to the glories displayed in the 104th Psalm, God was no longer in them; they were no longer His representations or 'names'. For He had now only one name— I AM—and that was participated by every being who had eyes that saw and ears that heard and who spoke through his throat. But it was incommunicable, because its participation by the particular self which is at this moment uttering it was an inseparable part of its meaning. Everyone can call his idol 'God', and many do; but no being who speaks through his throat can call a wholly other and outer Being 'I'.

Herein lay the mystery of the Divine Name. It was 'that name in which there is no participation between the Creator and any *thing* else'. So wrote the renowned Jewish Rabbi Maimonides in about the year 1190. And again:

> All the names of the Creator which are found in books are taken from his works, except one name, the Tetra-

grammaton, which is proper to him, and is therefore called 'the name apart' (*nomen separatum*); because it signifies the substance of the Creator by pure signification, in which there is no participation. His other glorious names do indeed signify by participation, because they are taken from his works.[1]

[1] Rabbi Moses ben Maimon. *Moreh Nebuhim*, (quoted by J. Drusius, a sixteenth-century scholar, in an essay on the *Tetragrammaton*).

# XVII

## THE DEVELOPMENT OF MEANING

In the course of this book many scattered references have been made to words and language. It is desirable that some attempt should now be made to draw the threads together.

When we are disputing about the proper meaning to be attached to a particular word in a sentence, etymology is of little use. Only children run to the dictionary to settle an argument. But if we would consider the *nature* of meaning, and the relation between thought and things, we cannot profitably dispense with etymology. It is long since men gave up the notion that the variety of natural species and the secrets of their relation to each other can be understood apart from their history; but many thinkers still seek to confine the science of language, as the Linnaeans once confined botany, within a sort of network of timeless abstractions. Method, for them, is another name for classification; but that is a blind alley.

Now etymology depicts the process of language in time. And it is a commonplace of the subject that, whatever word we hit on, if we trace its meaning far enough back, we find it apparently expressive of some tangible, or at all events, perceptible object or some physical activity. *Understanding* once meant 'standing under', and abstractions like *concept* and *hypothesis* merely disguise, in the garb of a dead language, a similarly humble origin. Even *right* and *wrong* are said to have once meant 'straight' and 'sour'.

In much more recent times we can observe the evolution

of a great deal of the emotional and psychological meaning in contemporary words out of an astrological, chemical, or physiological past. Many people are aware, without turning to a dictionary, of what *disposition, influence, melancholy,* etc., used to mean, and I have already referred in Chapter XII to the fact that similar changes are *still going on* in the case of such words as *heart* and *blood.* It would be in line with the general process of etymological change if, in future, the meaning of *heart* should become purely emotional, some other word such as *cardium* being appropriated to the physical organ.

Here and there, it is true, we may observe a change in the opposite direction; and it is certainly striking that the most abstract of all abstract terms—*relation*—should have become capable of signifying a solid, three-dimensional aunt or cousin. But these are the rare exceptions. Throughout the recorded history of language the movement of meaning has been from concrete to abstract.

I am here using the word 'abstract' in its broadest, and admittedly vague, sense, to cover everything in the familiar world we talk about, which is not, actually or theoretically, accessible to the senses; everything which a nineteenth-century logician would have termed an 'attribute'; and which some twentieth-century philosophers classify as a mere part of speech. In this sense *melancholy* and *a kind heart* may be as much abstractions as *concept* and *hypothesis*—it depends how we think of them. How we ought to think of them may be disputed, and indeed I am engaged in disputing it. But it is enough for my present purpose that nearly everybody to-day thinks of them as divorced from the 'appearances' of nature which are accessible to the senses—in a way which nearly everybody before the scientific revolution did not.

Systematic reflection on the *history* of language hardly began before the second half of the nineteenth century, when idolatry, as we have seen, was already near its culminating point; and when it had already, as described in Chapter IX, distorted the picture which men formed of the remote past. It was against this background, therefore, that the philologists of the nineteenth century sought to account for that unmistakable, semantic progress from concrete to abstract—or from 'outer' to 'inner'—to which I have just referred. In those circumstances, their answer to the problem was—metaphor. Before speech was invented, they said, primitive man lived in a world, except for details, very much like ours. His next step was to invent simple words for the simple things he saw about him—trees and animals, the sun and the moon, and so forth. And then, when his reason had evolved, and he found he needed words in which to express his inner life, he used these simple words again, but this time as metaphors. Herbert Spencer and Max Müller went further than this and added that, later on, men made the mistake of taking their own metaphors literally; and that this was the origin of mythology. Mythology, said Müller, is 'a disease of language'.

Of course, as time went on (they said), the metaphors 'faded'. We no longer call up any mental image of 'standing beneath', when we use the word *understand*, or of a physical 'pressing out', when we speak of *expressing* a sentiment or an idea. The progress was assumed to be from the metaphor, through the trope (which is a kind of moribund metaphor —as when we speak of following the *thread* of an argument), to the ordinary straightforward 'meaning'. But, whatever meanings its words might bear to-day, language was considered historically as a tissue of faded or dead metaphors.

Now there is no doubt that in the last few centuries the meanings of quite a number of the words with which we endeavour to express psychological facts or opinions *have* come into being in just this way—by deliberate transference from the outer world to the inner. *Emotion* is probably an example. But it is equally certain that the great majority have not. If we look into them, we find that they point us back, not to metaphor, but to participation; whether, like *disposition*, *influence*, and many others, through astrology, or whether, like *temper* and *humour*, through the old physiology, or whether, without being traceably connected with any particular system of thought, in one way or another they stem from a time before that exclusive disjunction between outer and inner, which the term 'metaphor' presupposes. Such is the case with many of the oldest words in the language—like *heart* and *blood*, to which I have already referred. Moreover, many much more recent words, to which a simple metaphorical origin may be hastily attributed, will be found on closer examination to betray similar birth-marks. *Depression*, for instance, would seem at first sight to be in the same class as *emotion*. But the evidence collected by the Oxford Dictionary suggests that its psychological significance did not, in fact, originate in a spatial metaphor (such as we use, when we speak of being 'on top of the world'), but as a literal discription of the state of the 'vital spirits'.

Many years ago, in a book called *Poetic Diction*, I drew attention to another fatal objection to this theory that words which to-day have a mental or emotional content acquired that content originally as a metaphorical extension of their meaning. It is this. If we find language growing more and more metaphorical, the further back we go into the past, what possible justification can there be for assuming a still earlier time when it was not metaphorical at all? Thus, Max Müller postulated a 'metaphorical period', during which the progress from literal to metaphorical meanings must have taken place. But, what is this but a purely arbitrary surmise? And is it not highly improbable? Why was such an assumption found necessary? Simply in order to make the evidence presented by the history of language fit in somehow or other with that 'evolution of idols', to which I have referred in Chapters V and IX.

It would take a very long time to trace all the influences exerted by preconceptions of this nature on the theories which men have formed about the origin and development of language, and even on lexicography itself. They are most easily detected by the train of inconsistencies they have left in their wake. Take, for instance, the old philological teaching of the building up of inflected and complex words from simple 'roots' of speech. Some languages, among which Hebrew is probably an outstanding example, are clearly formed about a relatively small number of consonant-groups consisting of three or even two letters each. Here is the bare fact. But what we make of it is all too likely to depend on the preconceptions with which we approach it. If we have preconceived a world in which the earliest speakers were surrounded by idols in all respects like our own, we shall treat these consonant-groups practically as 'words', and shall attribute to them meanings which were wide because they were generalized from particulars. This is what the philologists did; and it is particularly interesting to watch Max Müller relating this 'root' concept, as it was presented in his time, to his theory of a 'metaphorical period', to which I have already referred.

He invented a distinction between *radical* metaphor and *poetical* metaphor.

> I call it a radical metaphor when a root which means to shine is applied to form the names, not only of the fire or the sun, but of the spring of the year, the morning light, the brightness of thought, or the joyous outburst of hymns of praise. Ancient languages are brimful of such metaphors, and under the microscope of the etymologist almost every word discloses traces of its first metaphorical conception.

> From this we must distinguish *poetical* metaphor, namely, when a noun or verb, ready made and assigned to one definite object or action, is transferred poetically to another object or action. For instance, when the rays of the sun are called the hands or fingers of the sun.[1]

The assumption is, that men had on their lips the roots and in their minds the meanings, very much as we have words and their meanings to-day, and then proceeded to 'apply'

[1] *Science of Language*, p. 451.

them to a varied selection of phenomena. But, as was pointed out in the book already referred to,[1] this assumption is inconsistent in two respects with all that we know of primitive languages. Among very primitive and otherwise almost wordless peoples very short words are exactly what we do *not* find. Anthropologists tell us, instead, of the 'holophrase' or long, rambling conglomeration of sound and meaning. Words grow longer, not shorter, the nearer we get to the end of our backward journey towards the origin of speech. Secondly, a word meaning 'to shine' in general, as distinct from any particular kind of shining, is the very thing which a primitive mind is incapable of grasping. Indeed, much simpler generalizations, such as 'tree'—as distinct from a coconut-tree or a gum-tree—are equally beyond it. If, therefore, in any language the roots were there from the beginning, then, whatever else they were, they cannot have been words devised by men for the purpose of expressing general ideas.

I do not believe, then, that there is any such thing as a 'radical metaphor'. But I believe that reflection on the working of metaphor may nevertheless be a good approach to reflection on the nature of roots. For it is the peculiarity of metaphorical language that, at first sight, it does often resemble very closely the language of participation; though upon closer examination its existence is seen to depend precisely on the *absence* of participation.[2] It is at all events important to have made some such examination before we approach the wider question of the nature and origin of language.

[1] *Poetic Diction*, 2nd Edition, Faber 1952.    [2] Cf. p. 127.

# XVIII

## THE ORIGIN OF LANGUAGE

We have seen that, in the older doctrine of invented and applied 'roots of speech', as pointing to the origin of language, and in the more recent one of 'metaphor' as the principal instrument of the growth of meaning, we are saddled with two notions, which are both of them inconsistent with the testimony of language itself. If, on the other hand, we approach the history of meaning free from all assumptions based on biological theories of evolution; if we take our stand simply on a faithful study of the *nature* of language, then we shall not be seduced into any such arbitrary surmises. Instead, we shall be obliged to admit that 'metaphor' is a misleading concept to apply to any but the later and more sophisticated stages of language. For all the evidence points rather to that sort of 'polarization' of an ancient unity into an outer and an inner meaning, which was traced in Chapter XII. In other words, it points to the source of language in original participation—and, in doing so, indicates the direction in which we must look for a true understanding of those mysterious 'roots'. It is there, too, that we may hope in the end to espy the historical function of the word in determining the relation between thought and things.

We have seen that the difference between what I have called 'original' participation and the participation which can be grasped to-day in beta-thinking is, above all, a difference of direction. In the former, the represented is felt to be on the other side of the phenomena from the perceiving self. At the same time, it is felt to be linked with, or related to, that self otherwise than through the senses. The self, so far as there yet is one, is still aware that it and the phenomena derive from the same supersensible source. This kind of consciousness, then, is the subjective aspect of that coming-into-being, *pari passu*, of man and of his phenomena, which was referred to in Chapter X. Objectively, we could only describe the earlier stages of this process as a time when man—not only as a body, but also as a soul— was a part of nature in a way which we to-day, of course, find it difficult to conceive. Subjectively, he could not yet 'call his soul his own'. The farther back we penetrate, the more indistinguishable would his acts and utterances become from processes taking place in what has since become 'outer' nature.

It is conditions such as these which we must strive to realize in imagination, if we would hope to understand the 'root' element in language. Speech did not arise as the attempt of man to imitate, to master or to explain 'nature'; for speech and nature came into being along with one another. Strictly speaking, only idolators can raise the question of the 'origin of language'. For anyone else to do so is like asking for the origin of origin. Roots are the echo of nature herself sounding in man. Or rather, they are the echo of what once sounded and fashioned in both of them at the same time. And therefore it is, that they have always fascinated those adventurous souls—such as Fabre d'Olivet, Court de Gébelin or, in our own time, Herman Beckh, A. D. Wadler and others—who have sought to explore that difficult and perplexing territory—devasted as it has been by ensuing millennia of cultural divergence and etymological accidents— the relation between the sounds of language and its meanings.

The split between sound and meaning—for their relation in any modern language is no more than vestigial—is one aspect of the ever-widening gulf between outer and inner, phenomenon and name, thing and thought, with which this book is concerned. We have seen how that polarization into man : nature, which was the means to man's self-consciousness, was exaggerated by the scientific revolution into an exclusive disjunction. It was still a polarity, so long as *some* image-consciousness, *some* participation survived. We have seen also, in the preceding chapter, how the disjunction was deliberately purposed by the Jewish nation. I believe it will some day be realized that their mission was at the same time to prepare humanity against the day when it should be complete—that is, our own time.

The Hebrew language, through which (as we have seen) the inwardness of the Divine Name was later revealed, is at the same time, according to some opinions, that one among the ancient languages in which the roots preserve most clearly (though still dimly enough) the old unity of sound and meaning. If we try to think of these roots as 'words', then we must think of words with a potential rather than an actual meaning. Certainly those who have any feeling for sound-symbolism, and who wish to develop it, will be well advised to ponder them. They may find, in the consonantal element in language, vestiges of those forces which brought into being the external structure of nature, including the body of man; and, in the original vowel-sounds, the expression of that inner life of feeling and memory which constitutes his soul. It is the two together which have made possible, by first physically and then verbally embodying it, his personal intelligence.

The objective of this book is, however, a limited one, namely, to demonstrate on general grounds the necessity of smashing the idols. It cannot, therefore, attempt to investigate in detail what sort of knowledge may result from doing so, and it would be quite beyond its scope to carry this difficult subject any further. Suffice it to say that the Semitic languages seem to point us back to the old unity of man and nature, through the shapes of their sounds. We feel those shapes not only as sounds, but also, in a manner, as *gestures* of the speech-organs—and it is not so difficult to realize that these gestures were once gestures made with the whole body—once—when the body itself was not detached from the rest of nature after the solid manner of to-day, when the body itself was spoken even while it was speaking.

In an Aryan language, such as Greek, on the other hand, where natural and mythological significances so easily meet and mingle, we can feel more easily the nature of *phenomenal*—that is, imaginal—participation. The Aryan tongues point to the same ancient unity as the Semitic—but they do so through the quality of their *meaning*. Among the speakers of both types of language, a few centuries before the Christian era, a last faint echo of that unity appeared in the form of tradition and doctrine.

In the *Sefer Yezirah*, for instance, whose authorship was traditionally assigned to Abraham, and which was perhaps first committed to writing about A.D. 600, the account of creation given in the Book of Genesis is expanded, and related in considerable detail to the sounds and signs of a language at once divine and human. And the influence of the Jewish doctrine of the Word of God, which was at the same time the source of the phenomenal world and the incarnation of wisdom in man, is still clearly apparent in the Book of Proverbs and in the apocryphal *Ecclesiasticus* and *Wisdom of Solomon*. In the world of Greek thought the development in a similar direction, and particularly by the Stoic sect, of the *logos* of the Greek philosophers is better known; and it is an old story how the two streams met in Alexandria and united in a form which is probably best exemplified in the writings of Philo Judaeus.

All things came into being through the Word. This teaching of the creative Word, this last testimony to a creation which was not a mere creation of idols, and to an evolution which was not a mere evolution of idols, is one which Christian thought, thanks to the opening verses of St. John's Gospel, has never been able entirely to ignore, though it has by now come near to doing so. But the significance of this must be deferred to a later chapter.

# XIX

## SYMPTOMS OF ICONOCLASM

We have seen that the theory of metaphor, as the means by which language originally acquired its 'inner' meanings, is incorrect. But it is important to remember how it arose. It arose because there *is* a close relation between language as it is used by a participating consciousness and language as it is used, at a later stage, metaphorically or symbolically. When we use language metaphorically, we bring it about of our own free will that an appearance means something other than itself, and, usually, that a manifest 'means' an unmanifest. We start with an idol, and we ourselves turn the idol into a representation. We use the phenomenon as a 'name' for what is not phenomenal. And this, it will be remembered, is just what is characteristic of participation. Symbolism, as we saw in Chapter XI, is made possible by the elimination of participation. But at the end of Chapter XVI it was observed that in certain circumstances this may give rise to a new kind of participation—one which could no longer be described as 'original'.

What then has occurred? If we rapidly review the whole historical development of 'the word', we must say that, as soon as unconscious or subconscious organic processes have been sufficiently polarized to give rise to phenomena on the one side and consciousness on the other, *memory* is made possible. As consciousness develops into self-consciousness, the remembered phenomena become detached or liberated from their originals and so, as images, are in some measure at man's disposal. The more thoroughly participation has been eliminated, the more they are at the disposal of his imagination to employ as it chooses. If it chooses to impart its own meaning, it is doing, *pro tanto*, with the remembered phenomena what their Creator once did with the phenomena themselves. Thus there *is* a real analogy between metaphorical usage and original participation; but it is one which can only be acknowledged at this high, or even prophetic, level. It can only be acknowledged if the crude conception of an evolution of idols, which has dominated the last two centuries, is finally abandoned, or at all events is enlightened by one more in line with the old teaching of the Logos. There is a valid analogy *if*, but only if, we admit that, in the course of the earth's history, something like a Divine Word has been gradually clothing itself with the humanity it first gradually created—so that what was first spoken by God may eventually be respoken by man.

This granted, we can see how language, in the course of its history, has indeed mediated the transformation of phenomena into idols. But we can also see how, by reason of this very fact, *within* man the phenomena have gradually ceased to operate as compulsive natural processes and have become, instead, mere memory-images available for his own creative 'speech'—using 'speech' now in the wide sense of Aquinas's 'word'.

We should expect, accordingly, that, with the progressive decrease of participation throughout the Graeco-Roman, or Aristotelian age, we should find a growing awareness—however faint—of this capacity of man for creative speech. And we should expect to find a marked increase in that awareness after the scientific revolution. It is what we do find. Let us take, for example, the Romantic theory of the 'creative imagination' and glance briefly at its previous history. Premonitory hints of an attribution of 'creative' power to man as artist or poet, appear as early as the first Christian century, with Dio Chrysostom. A century later

Philostratus maintained of the works of Pheidias and Praxiteles, that:

> Imagination made them, and she is a better artist than imitation; for where the one carves only what she has seen, the other carves what she has not seen.

By the third century Plotinus is maintaining that:

> If anyone disparages the arts on the ground that they imitate nature, we must remind him that natural objects are themselves only imitations, and that the arts do not simply imitate what they see but reascend to those principles (λόγοι) from which Nature herself is derived.

For Scaliger in the sixteenth century (who was closely followed by Sidney in his *Apologie for Poesie*) the poet is one who 'maketh a new Nature and so maketh himself as it were a new God'.[1]

Coleridge's doctrine of the primary and secondary imagination, when it came, and the whole Romantic stress in England and Germany on the 'creative' function of art and poetry was, then, by no means a wholly new adventure in thought. It was rather that the whole attitude to nature, which it implied, had been rendered acceptable to a much wider circle by the rapidly increasing idolatry of the seventeenth and eighteenth centuries. Something very much like it had already been thought by a few. It became almost a popular movement in a world beginning at last to hunger for iconoclasm.

We have already had occasion to note the close relation between the apprehension of images and the making of them. As long as nature herself continued to be apprehended as image, it sufficed for the artist to imitate Nature. Inevitably, the life or spirit in the object lived on in his imitation, if it was a faithful one. For at the same time it could not help

---

[1] This important little piece of history will be found most effectively summarized at the beginning of Bk. III of Professor C. S. Lewis's *English Literature in the Sixteenth Century*. Clarendon Press. 1954.

being more than an imitation, inasmuch as the artist himself participated the being of the object. But the imitation of an *idol* is a purely technical process; which (as was quickly discovered) is better done by photography. To-day an artist cannot rely on the life inherent in the object he imitates, any more than a poet can rely on the life inherent in the words he uses. He has to draw the life forth from within himself.

It is for the same reason that an ever-increasing importance came to be attached to the *invented* image and men become more and more dissatisfied with imitations of nature both in the practice and in the theory of art. It is easy to see how it came to be held that 'the truest poetry is the most feigning'. For there is no doubt about where the life in an invented or fictitious image comes from. There can be no 'pathetic fallacy' there. What is peculiar to the Romantic Movement—as, indeed, its very name recalls—is the further reaction of this enthusiasm for fictitious and *fabulous* representations on the phenomena—on Nature herself. This is also what took the Romantic conception of art, properly understood, a step beyond the Neo-platonic theory referred to above. The Neo-platonic theory holds that man the artist is, in some measure, a creator. The Romantic conception agrees—but goes further and returns him, in this capacity, to Nature herself.

With what result? It is no longer simply that the arts 're-ascend to those principles from which nature herself is derived'. The 'principles' themselves have changed their venue. For we are told by the Romantic theory that we must no longer look for the nature-spirits—for the Goddess Natura—on the farther side of the appearances; we must look for them *within ourselves*.

> *Unbewusst der Freuden, die sie schenket,*
> *Nie entzückt von ihrer Herrlichkeit,*
> *Nie gewahr des Geistes, der sie lenket,*
> *Sel'ge nur durch meine Seligkeit,*

# Symptoms of Iconoclasm

*Fühllos selbst für ihres Künstlers Ehre,*
*Gleich dem toten Schlag der Pendeluhr,*
*Dient sie knechtisch dem Gesetz der Schwere,*
*Die entgötterte Natur.*[1]

Pan has shut up shop. But he has not retired from business; he has merely gone indoors. Or, in the well-known words of Coleridge:

> *We receive but what we give*
> *And in our life alone does Nature live.*[2]

It is again beyond the scope of this book to trace in detail the way in which the origin of the Romantic response to nature is exemplified in that association between Coleridge and Wordsworth which gave rise to the *Lyrical Ballads*. It was the dejected author of the *Ancient Mariner* who grasped the theory; but it was Wordsworth who actually *wrote* the nature-poetry.

If nature is indeed 'dis-godded', and yet we again begin to experience her, as Wordsworth did—and as millions have done since his time—no longer as dead but as alive; if there is no 'represented' on the far side of the appearances, and yet we begin to experience them once more *as* appearances, as representations—the question arises, of *what* are they representations? It was no doubt the difficulty of answering this question which led Wordsworth to relapse occasionally into that nostalgic hankering after *original* participation, which is called pantheism—and from which Coleridge was rendered immune by his acquaintance with Kantian philosophy. We shall find somewhat the same contrast, in this respect, between Goethe and Schiller.

It is because of its failure to answer this question that the true, one might say the tremendous, impulse underlying the

[1] From Schiller's *Die Götter Griechenlands*: 'Unconscious of the joy she bestows, never transported by her own glory, never aware of the spirit that directs her, blest only through my blessedness, without feeling even for the honour of her artist—as with the dead stroke of a clock's pendulum she—disgodded Nature—slavishly obeys the law of gravity.'
[2] *Ode to Dejection.*

Romantic movement has never grown to maturity; and, after adolescence, the alternative to maturity is puerility. There is only one answer to the question. Henceforth, if nature is to be experienced as representation, she will be experienced as representation of—Man. But what is Man? Herein lies the direst possibility inherent in idolatry. It can empty of spirit—it has very nearly succeeded in doing so—not only nature, but also Man himself. For among all the other idols is his own body. And it is part of the creed of idolatry that, when we speak of Man, we mean only the body of this or that man, or at most his finite personality, which we are driven more and more to think an attribute of his body.

Thus it is, that the great change which the evolution of consciousness has brought about and the great lessons which men had begun to learn have all been wrenched awry. We had come at last to the point of realizing that art can no longer be content with imitating the collective representations, now that these are themselves turning into idols. But, instead of setting out to smash the idols, we have tamely concluded that nothing can now be art which in any way reminds us of nature—and even that practically anything may be art, which does not. We have learned that art can represent nothing but Man himself, and we have interpreted that as meaning that art exists for the purpose of enabling Mr. Smith to 'express his personality'. And all because we have not learnt—though our very physics shouts it at us—that nature herself is the representation of Man.

Hence the riot of private and personal symbolisms into which both art and poetry have degenerated. If I know that nature herself is the system of my representations, I cannot do otherwise than adopt a humbler and more responsible attitude to the representations of art and the metaphors of poetry. For in the case of nature there is no danger of my fancying that she exists to express my personality. I know in that case that what is meant, when I say she is my representation, is, that I stand, whether I like it or not, in—(I do not love the expression, but I can find no defter one in English) a 'directionally creator' relation to her. But I know also that what so stands is not my poor temporal personality, but the Divine Name in the unfathomable depths behind it. And if I strive to produce a work of art, I cannot then do otherwise than strive humbly to create more nearly as *that* creates, and not as my idiosyncrasy wills.

After all, there is warrant for it. At the beginning of the first chapter I pointed to the phenomenon of the rainbow, because it is especially easy there to realize the extent to which it is 'our' creation. But we know equally well that it is not only the colours and curve of the rainbow which proceed from the eye; it is not only 'Iris' who has gone indoors; we know that light itself—*as light* (whatever we may think about the particles)—proceeds from the same source. Now for the Impressionist painters, this became a real experience. They really painted nature in the light of the eye, as no other painters had done before them. They were striving to realize in consciousness the normally unconscious activity of 'figuration' itself. They did not imitate; they expressed 'themselves'—inasmuch as they painted nature as the representation of Man. They will serve as a reminder—though they are not the only one—that the rejection of original participation may mean, not the destruction but the liberation of images.

## XX

## FINAL PARTICIPATION

I referred in Chapter XIII to symbolism as something in which we to-day are again becoming interested. There is no respect in which the imaginative literature and drama of to-day differs more strikingly from that of even fifty years ago. In those days there was an Ibsen, there was a Maeterlinck, but nobody really understood what they were up to and everyone was dubious and uncomfortable. Whereas to-day every other writer strives to imply some sort of symbolized content and, even if he does not, it is obligingly done for him by confident critics who have read their Freud and their Jung. It would be an interesting experiment to resuscitate a habitual reader of, say, the *Times Literary Supplement* in the 'nineties, to set him down before the second half of the *New Statesman* in the 1950's, and to see what he made of it.

In mentioning Freud and Jung I have, of course, touched on the most startling phenomenon of all. The unaccountable rapidity with which a literal-minded generation developed a sympathetic response to the psycho-analytical gnosis of dream-imagery, and accepted the (one would have thought) fantastic idea of an immaterial realm of 'the unconscious', is another sign, in addition to those I instanced in Chapter X, that the development of man's consciousness is an evolutionary as well as a dialectical process. Who could possibly have foreseen it in the year of the Great Exhibition? Who could have failed to deny the possibility of such a change, if it had been foretold to him? Possibly the greatest, possibly the only lasting, value of psycho-analysis lies in its clinical aspect. It may or may not be so. But for the historian of consciousness the most significant thing will always be the way it 'caught on'; the number of its technical terms—and still more the characters out of Greek mythology—which had become household words even before the death of its founder. Pan, it seems, has not only not retired from business; he has not only gone indoors; he has hardly shut the door, before we begin to hear him moving about inside.

Yet here again, as far as any extra-clinical value is concerned, the historian of the future will observe the fatally blighting influence of the conventional idolatry. It never seems to have even occurred to Freud that an individual man's 'unconscious mind' could be anything but a 'somewhat' lodged inside the box of his bones. Representation, as a principle, is accepted by him as a matter of course; inasmuch as a great variety of dream-imagery is interpreted as symbolizing particular physical functions. From the perception that physical functions and organs are *themselves* representations, he is, however, cut off by all the assumptions of idolatry. Again, we have watched with interest Jung developing his concept of a 'collective unconscious' of humanity as a whole, a concept which is inherently repugnant to the foundation of idolatry on which he had to build it. Yet, because of that very idolatry, the traditional myths and the archetypes which he tells us are the representations of the collective unconscious, are assumed by him to be, and always to have been, neatly insulated from the world of nature with which, according to their own account, they were mingled or united.

The psychological interpretation of mythology is, it is true, a long way nearer to an understanding of participation than the old 'personified causes' of Tylor and Frazer and Lemprière's Classical Dictionary. But it is still a long way off. In the last resort, when it actually comes up against the nature-content of the myths, it still relies on the old anthropological assumption of 'projection'. I believe it will seem very strange to the historian of the future, that a literal-minded generation began to accept the actuality of a 'collective unconscious' before it could even admit the possibility of a 'collective conscious'—in the shape of the phenomenal world.

I do not, however, think it can be very long now before this, too, is accepted; since it not only opens up possibilities of new knowledge of which the need is being increasingly felt, but also removes many inconsistencies in the contemporary picture of the world, which cannot fail to be noticed more and more as time passes. Idolatry carries in it the seeds of its own destruction. The reader will, for instance, recall the dilemma of 'pre-history' which was briefly touched on in Chapter V. We have chosen to form a picture, based very largely on modern physical science, of a phenomenal earth existing for millions of years before the appearance of consciousness. The same physical science tells us that the phenomenal world is correlative to consciousness. The phenomena attributed to these millions of years are therefore, in fact, abstract models or 'idols of the study'. We may compromise by calling them 'possible phenomena', implying thereby that that was how the world would have looked, sounded, smelt and felt, *if* there had been someone like ourselves present. But if the only phenomena we know are collective representations, and what is represented is the collective unconscious, the awkward fact remains that it is highly fanciful, if not absurd, to think of any unperceived process in terms of potential phenomena, unless we also assume an unconscious, ready to light up into actual phenomena at any moment of the process.

This of course applies not only to pre-history, but to all the imperceptible process assumed in our picture of the contemporary world—the goings-on, for instance, at the bottom of the sea. But in the case of pre-history, we have further to remember that it does not suffice to accept the reality of a collective unconscious *now*. We have to accept that an unconscious, available to be represented, is at least coeval with any process describable in terms of phenomena. The employment of 'models' for the purpose of thinking may be very well; for the purposes of exposition it may even be essential—as long as we know what we are doing and do not turn the models into idols. And we shall know what we are doing with pre-history, when we have firmly grasped the fact that the phenomenal world arises from the relation between a conscious and an unconscious and that evolution is the story of the changes that relation has undergone and is undergoing.

But it is not only for the study of pre-history that it is all-important for us to realize this truth, that the phenomena are collective representations of what can *now* properly be called 'man's' unconscious. It is vital for the future of the sciences, especially those at the other end of the scale from the technological ones—those, in short, for which 'dash-board-knowledge'[1] is not enough. When, for instance, we are dealing with living organisms, our whole approach, our whole possibility of grasping *process* as such, is hamstrung by the lack of just such a concept of the potentially pheno-menal and the actually phenomenal.

With the help of the Arabian schoolmen the Aristotelian concept of 'potential' existence was gradually drained away into the mere notional 'possibility' of being—into *contingent* being. Thus, the word *potentialis* (itself a translation of the vigorous Greek word from which we take our 'dynamic' and 'dynamite') had been changed to *possibilis* before Aquinas wrote, though his *possibilis* still meant more than our 'possible'. Since the scientific revolution, to ask whether a thing 'is' or 'is not' is, for science, to ask whether it is or is not a phenomenon—either experienced or extrapolated. Francis Bacon, it will be remembered, found the distinction between *actus* and *potentia* 'frigida distinctio'; and so it had to be, while the phenomena were becoming, and will be as long as they remain, idols. But to-day, it is no longer open

[1] Cf. p. 55.

to anyone who regards the unconscious as more than a fiction to contend that the concept of the potentially phenomenal, that is, of potential existence, is too difficult for human minds to grasp.

Even so, merely grasping the concept will not take mankind very far. Beta-thinking can go thus far. It can convince itself that, just as for original participation potential existence was something quite different from not-being, so, for the kind of participation at which we have arrived to-day, the potentially phenomenal is not the same as nothing. Let us call the man-centred participation with which the opening chapters of this book were concerned *final participation*. Beta-thinking, then, can convince itself of the *fact* of final participation. It can convince itself that we participate the phenomena with the unconscious part of ourselves. But that has no epistemological significance. It can only have that to the extent that final participation is consciously experienced. Perhaps (if we may already start using the old terminology which we have just taken out of the refrigerator) we may say that final participation must itself be raised from potentiality to act.

Are there any signs of such a development taking place? We have seen, in the Romantic movement, and elsewhere, symptoms of a kind of instinctive impulse towards iconoclasm. Are there any signs up to now of a *systematic* approach to final participation? And what does such an approach involve?

It was pointed out in Chapter XIII that participation as an actual experience is only to be won to-day by special exertion; that it is a matter, not of theorizing, but of imagination in the genial or creative sense. A systematic approach towards final participation may therefore be expected to be an attempt to use imagination systematically. This was the foundation of Goethe's scientific work. In his book on the *Metamorphosis of Plants* and the associated writings descriptive of his method, as well as in the rest of his scientific work, there is the germ of a systematic investigation of phenomena by way of participation. For his *Urpflanze* and *Urphänomen* are nothing more or less than potential phenomena perceived and studied as such. They are processes grasped directly and not, as hitherto since the scientific revolution, hypotheses *inferred from* actual phenomena.

I have here used both the word 'scientific' and the word 'perceived' advisedly, though in such a context both of them run counter to all the assumptions of the received idolatry. It is a common objection that Goethe's method ought not to be called 'scientific', because it was not purely empirical; but that objection obviously cannot be raised here without begging the whole argument of this book. As to 'perceived'—we have seen that the major part of any perceived phenomenon consists of our own 'figuration'. Therefore, as imagination reaches the point of enhancing figuration itself, hitherto unperceived parts of the whole field of the phenomenon necessarily become perceptible. Moreover, this conscious participation enhances perception not only of present phenomena but also of the memory-images derived from them. All this Goethe could not prevail on his contemporaries to admit. Idolatry was too all-powerful and there were then no premonitory signs, as there are to-day, of its collapse. No one, for instance, had heard of 'the unconscious'.

For a student of the evolution of consciousness, it is particularly interesting that a man with the precise make-up of Goethe should have appeared at that precise moment in the history of the West. By the middle of the eighteenth century, when he was born, original participation had virtually faded out, and Goethe himself was a thoroughly modern man. Yet he showed from his earliest childhood and retained all through his life an almost atavistically strong remainder of it. It breathes through his poetry as the peculiar Goethean attitude to Nature, who is felt as a living being, almost as a personality, certainly as a 'thou' rather than as an 'it' or an 'I'. It is almost as if the Gods had purposely retained this sense in Goethe as a sort of seed-corn out of which the beginnings of final participation could peep, for the first time, on the world of science. Perhaps it was an instinctive understanding of this which made him so determined to keep clear of beta-thinking.

> *Mein kind, ich hab' es klug gemacht,*
> *Ich hab' nie über das Denken gedacht.*[1]

For beta-thinking leads to final, by way of the inexorable elimination of all original, participation. Consequently Goethe was able to develop an elementary technique, but unable, or unwilling, to erect a metaphysic, of final participation. The contrast in this respect between him and Schiller, who knew his Kant and stood firm in the idolatry of his contemporaries—especially as it appeared in a certain conversation[2] between the two on the subject of the *Urphänomen*—is illuminating and is in a manner, as I have said, analogous to the contrast between Wordsworth and Coleridge. There is, so far as I know, more of the historical *theory* of participation in Schiller's poem *Die Götter Griechenlands* (from which I have already quoted in Chapter XIX) than in anything Goethe ever wrote. Yet Schiller could not admit the practical possibility of final participation at all. He told Goethe that his *Urphänomen* was no more than an idea, a hypothesis; and the poem itself, after a magnificent account of the retreat of the Gods from nature into man, has nothing more significant or prophetic to conclude with than the rather trite:

> *Was unsterblich im Gesang soll leben*
> *Muss im Leben untergehen.*[3]

The significance of Goethe in the history of science will be appreciated, as time passes, in the measure that idolatry is overcome. His theory of colour, for instance, will always

[1] 'I have managed things cleverly, my boy: I have never thought about thinking.' *Zahme Xenien*, vi.

[2] *Naturwissenschaftliche Schriften* (*Kürschner-Ausgabe*). Vol. i, p. 109; Appendices to the *Metamorphosenlehre* (*Glückliches Ereignis*).

[3] 'What is to live immortal in song must go under in life.'

be heterodox as long as the phenomenon of light is simply identified with the unrepresented 'particles'. But that significance, however great it may ultimately appear, grows pale before the significance of Rudolf Steiner (1861–1925) who, in the early part of his life, studied and developed the method of Goethe. Unlike Goethe, however, Steiner did not avoid beta-thinking. At the same time that he was editing Goethe's scientific works in Weimar, he was writing his book *The Philosophy of Spiritual Activity*, in which the metaphysic of final participation is fully and lucidly set forth. Educated on 'the modern side' (as we should then have said) at school and university, he was thoroughly at home with the idols and never relied on any relic of original participation there may have been in his composition to overcome them. It is in his work and that of his followers that the reader should look for further signs of a development towards final participation in the field of science.

If a single example is sought, let it be the research now going on in the domain of cancer. Cancer is a process of generation, and once we admit the concept of the potentially phenomenal, we must see that generation is not a transition from not-being to being, but a transition from potential to phenomenal existence. Steiner's method, based on perception of the potentially phenomenal, was to diagnose a pre-cancerous condition of the blood, a condition not yet detectable by physical symptoms, and thus to take the disease at a stage where it answers better to treatment. This is another way of saying that the method involves investigation of a part of the field of the whole phenomenon named *blood* which, for a non-participating consciousness, is excluded from it, not by empirical proof but rather (as we saw in Chapter XII) by definition. He sought to apply the same method to the discovery of remedies, and The Society for Cancer Research founded by his followers is patiently continuing this difficult work at Arlesheim in Switzerland. At the moment in which I am writing, however, more people are probably acquainted with the 'Biodynamic' method in Agriculture than with the particular example I have chosen.

The mind of Rudolf Steiner was of course not only applied to the scientific sphere, and it was perhaps not even the most important part of his work. He is, for instance, far more illuminating and, I would say, reliable on the subject of language and its origin than Fabre d'Olivet and the others I mentioned in Chapter XVIII. To say that he advocated, and practised, 'the systematic use of imagination' is to place so much emphasis on the mere beginning of what he taught and did, that it is rather like saying that Dante wrote a poem about a greyhound. Steiner showed that imagination, and the final participation it leads to, involve, unlike hypothetical thinking, the whole man—thought, feeling, will, and character—and his own revelations were clearly drawn from those further stages of participation— Inspiration and Intuition—to which the systematic use of imagination may lead. Although the object with which this book was originally conceived was none other than to try and remove one of the principal obstacles to contemporary appreciation of precisely this man's teaching—the study and use of which I believe to be crucial for the future of mankind—I shall here say no more of it. This is a study in idolatry, not a study of Rudolf Steiner.[1]

[1] All the published works of Rudolf Steiner are obtainable in London, either in English translation or in the original German, from:

Rudolf Steiner Book Shop, 35 Park Road, N.W.1. or Rudolf Steiner Book Centre, 54 Bloomsbury St., W.C.1.

# XXI

## SAVING THE APPEARANCES

It may be well, before proceeding further, to restate very briefly what this book has so far endeavoured to establish. It has been sought to show firstly, that the evolution of nature is correlative to the evolution of consciousness; and, secondly, that the evolution of consciousness hitherto can best be understood as a more or less continuous progress from a vague but immediate awareness of the 'meaning' of phenomena towards an increasing preoccupation with the phenomena themselves. The earlier awareness involved experiencing the phenomena as representations; the latter preoccupation involves experiencing them, non-representationally, as objects in their own right, existing independently of human consciousness. This latter experience, in its extreme form, I have called *idolatry*.

Idolatry is an ugly and emphatic word and it was deliberately chosen to emphasize certain ugly features, and still more certain ugly possibilities, inherent in the present situation. Not much has been said of the benefits—not only material ones—which have been conferred on mankind by this 'idolatry' and nothing, as yet, of the supreme benefit, which will be dealt with in the final chapters. As to the former, most people are so well aware of these benefits, and they have been so often and so fully emphasized by others, that I have thought it unnecessary to draw attention to them. But I will mention two at this point. In the first place, together with the ability to experience phenomena as objects independent of human consciousness, there has grown up our enormously improved power of grasping them in exact and quantitative detail. (Indeed, it was by shifting our attention to this detail that we gained that ability.) With this has come the progressive elimination of those errors and confusions in which alpha-thinking is inevitably entangled while, in its initial stages, it is still over-shadowed by participation; that is, the vague but immediate awareness of 'meaning' already referred to. And with this again, has come the power of effective manipulation on which our civilization, with its many works of mercy, is based. Surgery, for example, presupposes an acquaintance with the human anatomy exact in the same mode that our knowledge of a machine is exact.

Yet these practical considerations are not the only ones. Along with his idolatry, and because of it, modern man has found the possibility of an entirely new and very charming emotional relation to nature. The devoted love which thousands of naturalists, for example, have felt for some aspect of nature to which they have been drawn, is not in spite of, it is actually *dependent* on their experience of the 'appearances' as substantially independent of themselves. The whole joy of it depends on its being an 'I—it' relation —oblivious, or contemptuous, of the teleological approach which dominated Aristotle and the Middle Ages. The happy bird-watcher does not say: 'Let's go and see what we can learn about ourselves from nature'. He says: 'Let's go and see what nature is doing, bless her!' Without idolatry there would have been no Gilbert White, no Richard Jefferies, no W. H. Hudson, no Lorenz. Nor is this emotional relation confined to the naturalists, professional and amateur. They are merely the most striking example. The possibility of a selfless and attentive love for birds, animals, flowers, clouds, rocks, water, permeates the whole modern mind, its science, its art, its poetry and its daily life. It is something which only a fool would be in a hurry to sacrifice.

On the other hand, precisely if we are *not* fools, our very love of natural phenomena 'for their own sake' will be enough to prevent us from hastily turning a blind eye on any new light which can be shed, from any direction whatsoever, on their true nature. Above all will this be the case, if we feel them to be in danger. And if the appearances are, as I have sought to establish, correlative to human consciousness and if human consciousness does not remain unchanged but evolves, then the future of the appearances, that is, of nature herself, must indeed depend on the direction which that evolution takes.

Now in considering future possibilities there are, it has been suggested, two opposing tendencies to be taken into consideration. On the one hand, a further development in the direction, and on the basis, of idolatry; involving in the end the elimination of those last vestiges of original participation, which, as we saw in Chapter XV, survive in our language and therefore in our collective representations. On the other hand, there is the impulse, rudimentary as yet, of the human imagination to substitute for original participation, a different kind of participation, which I have called 'final'. This, we saw, is based on the acceptance (mainly impulsive so far, but occasionally explicit) of the fact that man himself now stands in a 'directionally creator relation'[1] to the appearances. It would seem that the appearances are in danger from both quarters, and that they will require 'saving', in a rather different sense of the term from that used of old by Simplicius.

The plain fact is, that all the unity and coherence of nature depends on participation of one kind or the other. If therefore man succeeds in eliminating all original participation, without substituting any other, he will have done nothing less than to eliminate all meaning and all coherence from the cosmos. We have seen that here and there he is already beginning an attempt to eliminate meaning—that is, a valid relation to nature—from his language, and there-

[1] Cf. p. 132.

with striking a blow at the very roots of his collective representations. Less sensationally, but far more effectively and over a much wider area, his science, with the progressive disappearance of original participation, is losing its grip on any principle of unity pervading nature as a whole and the knowledge of nature. The hypothesis of chance has already crept from the theory of evolution into the theory of the physical foundation of the earth itself; but, more serious perhaps than that, is the rapidly increasing 'fragmentation of science' which occasionally attracts the attention of the British Association. There is no 'science of sciences'; no unity of knowledge. There is only an accelerating increase in that pigeon-holed knowledge by individuals of more and more about less and less, which, if persisted in indefinitely, can only lead mankind to a sort of 'idiocy' (in the original sense of the word)—a state of affairs, in which fewer and fewer representations will be collective, and more and more will be private, with the result that there will in the end be no means of communication between one intelligence and another.

The second danger arises from final participation itself. Imagination is not, as some poets have thought, simply synonymous with good. It may be either good or evil. As long as art remained primarily mimetic, the evil which imagination could do was limited by nature. Again, as long as it was treated as an amusement, the evil which it could do was limited in scope. But in an age when the connection between imagination and figuration is beginning to be dimly realized, when the fact of the directionally creator relation is beginning to break through into consciousness, both the good and the evil latent in the working of imagination begin to appear unlimited. We have seen in the Romantic movement an instance of the way in which the making of images may react on the collective representations. It is a fairly rudimentary instance, but even so it has already gone beyond the dreams and responses of a leisured few. The economic and social structure of Switzerland, for example, is noticeably affected by its tourist industry, and that is due only in part to increased facilities of travel. It is due not less to the fact that (whatever may be said about their 'particles') the *mountains* which twentieth-century man sees are not the mountains which eighteenth-century man saw.

It may be objected that this is a very small matter, and that it will be a long time before the imagination of man substantially alters those appearances of nature with which his figuration supplies him. But then I am taking the long view. Even so, we need not be too confident. Even if the pace of change remained the same, one who is really sensitive to (for example) the difference between the medieval collective representations and our own will be aware that, without travelling any greater distance than we have come since the fourteenth century, we could very well move forward into a chaotically empty or a fantastically hideous world. But the pace of change has *not* remained the same. It has accelerated and is accelerating.

We should remember this, when appraising the aberrations of the formally representational arts. Of course, in so far as these are due to affectation, they are of no importance. But in so far as they are genuine, they are genuine because the artist has in some way or other experienced the world he represents. And in so far as they are appreciated, they are appreciated by those who are themselves willing to make a move towards seeing the world in that way, and, ultimately therefore, seeing that kind of world. We should remember this, when we see pictures of a dog with six legs emerging from a vegetable marrow or a woman with a motor-bicycle substituted for her left breast.

The systematic use of imagination, then, will be requisite in the future, not only for the increase of knowledge, but also for saving the appearances from chaos and inanity. Nor need it involve any relinquishment of the ability which we have won to experience and love nature as objective and independent of ourselves. Indeed, it cannot involve that.

For any such relinquishment would mean that what was taking place was not an approach towards final participation (which is the proper goal of imagination) but an attempt to revert to original participation (which is the goal of pantheism, of mediumism and of much so-called occultism). To be *able* to experience the representations as idols, and then to be able also to perform the act of figuration consciously, so as to experience them as participated; that is imagination.

The extremity of idolatry towards which we are moving renders the attainment of this dual relation to nature a necessity for both art and science. The attempt to unite the voluntary creativity demanded by the one with the passive receptivity demanded by the other is the significance of Goethe's contribution to the Western mind, as the achievement of it is the significance of Rudolf Steiner's. It is perhaps still not too late to attend to these portents. The appearances will be 'saved' only if, as men approach nearer and nearer to conscious figuration and realize that it is something which may be affected by their choices, the final participation which is thus being thrust upon them is exercised with the profoundest sense of responsibility, with the deepest thankfulness and piety towards the world as it was originally given to them in original participation, and with a full understanding of the momentous process of history, as it brings about the emergence of the one from the other.

# XXII

## SPACE, TIME AND WISDOM

The Western type of consciousness may be said to have begun, as we saw at the end of Chapter XV, with the emergence of Greek thought from the Orient. For the Western outlook is based essentially on that turning of man's *attention* to the phenomena, which in this book has been called alpha-thinking. This is sharply contrasted with the oriental impulse (still heard echoing on in Plato) to *refrain* from the phenomena, to remain, as it were, in the bosom of the Eternal, to disregard as irrelevant to man's true being, all *that*, in his experience, which is based on 'the contacts of the senses'. Oriental philosophy, hardly distinguishable from oriental theology, is based, above all, on a determination to regard the sense-world as *Maya*, or illusion. It was for this reason that, on its rediscovery in the nineteenth century, it made such a strong appeal to the few who were by then becoming dimly aware that the enlightenment of the West is based on idolatry. It is clear, however, that the way of the West lies, not back but forward; not in withdrawal from the contacts of the senses, but in their transformation and redemption.

We have also seen that the rise and growth of alpha-thinking was associated with a change in man's experience of space. It was with difficulty that *movement*, and particularly movement in a circle, was first wholly distinguished from mental activity; and this applied especially to the celestial revolutions, which were approached in a way that suggests that what we call space was conceived rather as a kind of unindividualized, all-enclosing continuum, or mental *mobile*, for which perhaps *wisdom* is the best modern word we can find. Space, as a mindless, wisdomless, lifeless void, was not a common notion at any time before the scientific revolution; thus at the close of Chapter XI we saw how the experience of space differed from our own, even as recently as medieval times. To the remnant of participation which then still survived, man, as microcosm, was placed at the centre of the macrocosm; but the point was, that he was an *organic* centre. The spatial aspect of the relation was incidental. It is only when space itself has become an idol—when it has become simply *the absence of phenomena, conceived in the phenomenal mode*—that perspective takes the place of participation. For the mode of vision which perspective reproduces, each pair of eyes is placed at the centre of a purely spatial sphere, and any organic relation there may be is incidental.

If therefore we should wish to revive in ourselves the faculty of experiencing spatial form as representation, and if we should wish to seek assistance in doing so, from the past history of man, we shall do well to look backwards to the East, along the path that led through the Greeks to the scientific revolution.

We have seen however that there is another line along which we can also look back to the same source. In Chapter XVI we saw that, long before the alpha-thinking of the Greeks had begun its long task of eliminating participation from human consciousness, the Jewish nation, with a different impulse and a more considered purpose, had initiated the like process. In their case there was no question of turning their attention to the phenomenon for its own sake, or at all. The killing out of participation was the end, in itself, and imagery of all kinds was the quarry marked out for destruction.

It has often been pointed out that we find reflected in the early literature of the Jews an entirely new feeling for the significance of history, and perhaps of time itself. It is in their apocalypses that we first detect a conception of history as something which had a beginning and is moving towards an end. The apocalypses have even been pointed to as the earliest example of something that could be called a doctrine of evolution. It has perhaps not been so often remarked that a peculiar sense of the significance and shape of time is also reflected in the Hebrew language. Not only, for example, does the Hebrew verb possess no present tense, as we understand it in the Aryan languages; the past being used for every moment up to the present, and the future for every moment from the present on. Not only is this the case, but the past and future are interchangeable in ways which it is difficult for us to understand. More than one Hebrew grammarian, for instance, has declared that the past tense was used for prophecy and the future for history.

Once again we notice a sharp contrast with what had gone before. The oriental conception of time was essentially cyclic. The picture was one of eternal repetition rather than of beginning, progress and end, and the path of the individual soul to the bosom of eternity was a backward path of extrication from the wheels of desire in which it had allowed itself to become involved. To reach, or to resume, the Supreme Identity with Brahma, with the Eternal, was the object and its achievement was a matter which lay directly between the individual and the Eternal. The Semitic way, on the other hand, was a way forward through history and it was a way, shared indeed by the individual, but trodden by the nation as a whole.

In a study such as this, which necessarily attempts to cover a great deal of ground in a very short space, one should beware of overstressing a resemblance to make a neat parallel. But I think it is true to say that, just as by looking back through the Greek mind, we bring to life the apprehension of form in space as an image or representation, so, by looking back through the Jewish mind, we bring to life the apprehension of form in time—that is, of events themselves, as images, whether of the past or future, or of a state of mind.

The second is a far more difficult achievement for us than the first. But I believe that anyone who would well consider the way of experiencing Old Testament history, which is implied in the Psalms and in the Jewish liturgy, and then again in Christian art before the Reformation, would understand what I mean. To immerse oneself in the medieval Mystery plays and in those sequences and parallels between Old and New Testament, which are the very backbone, the essential formal principle of the Cathedral sculptures, is to feel that, in one most real sense, the Old Testament was lost with the Reformation.

For non-participating consciousness it is either, or. A narrative is *either* a historical record, *or* a symbolical representation. It cannot be both; and the pre-figurings of the New Testament in the Old, and the whole prophetic element in the Old Testament is now apt to be regarded as moonshine. In a parallel sphere, however—the life-history of the individual man—it is already no longer taken quite so confidently for granted that the historical and the symbolical are contradictories. In the nineteenth century it required the powerful imagination of a John Keats to perceive that 'every man's life is a perpetual allegory'. In our own day the development of psychology alone has made this possible for much more ordinary men. Though not many may agree with him, a man is no longer regarded as a lunatic, who divines that the things which happen to a person, and the order in which they happen, may be as much a part of him as his physical organism. And it seems to lie in the natural order of things that, with the further increase of final participation, this perception should be extended to the biographies of nations and races, and of humanity as a whole.

All things considered, before we reject out of hand the possibility of any imaginal principle in time and the events of history, we should do well to consider how we are getting on with our own conception both of time and of space.

The concept of space as an unlimited or three-dimensional void—a kind of extrapolated 'perspective'—which came in with the disappearance of participation, is still of course the ordinary man's concept. It held good for science, too, until the end of the nineteenth century. The indications that it is now proving inadequate are so numerous that I do not need to stress them. When, for instance, we are told that space must be conceived as spherical, or asked to think in terms of a 'space-time continuum', we can hardly avoid the conclusion that the old, or rather the still young, 'idol' of infinity as a 'going on for ever', whether in space or time, is showing unmistakable signs of strain. There seems to be a strong tendency, both in dealing with the periphery and in dealing with the centre of the physical universe, to substitute what are in effect thought-patterns for plausible and seriously supposed spatial apparatus. Is not the rather hectic picture of a universe expanding in all directions with almost infinite rapidity, in essence a geometrical rather than a physical notion? I am told at all events that it bears a marked resemblance to projective geometry. 'It appears,' said Lord Russell, broadcasting in April 1955 on the death of Einstein,

> that the universe is of finite size, although unbounded. (Do not attempt to understand this unless you have studied non-Euclidean geometry.) It appears also that the universe is continually getting bigger.

We turn from the periphery to the infinitesimal centre of our 'perspectivized' space, and we hear the same voice in the same broadcast assuring us that:

> Nobody before quantum theory doubted that at any given moment a particle is at some definite place and moving with some definite velocity. This is no longer the case. The more accurately you determine the place of a particle, the less accurate will be its velocity; and the more accurately you determine the velocity, the less accurate

will be its position. And the particle itself has become something quite vague, not a nice little billiard ball as it used to be. When you think you have caught it, it produces a convincing alibi as a wave and not a particle. In fact, you know only certain equations of which the interpretation is obscure.

The reader will be aware that in this book I have called that 'something quite vague' by the name either of 'the particles' or of 'the unrepresented' and have then, for reasons given, largely dismissed it from consideration. This is perhaps the place to say a final word about it. Physical science postulates an unrepresented, as a something which is independent of our consciousness in a way, or to an extent to which the phenomena are not. Our consciousness is, however, not independent of *it*; for it is in response to its stimulus that our senses and our figuration and thinking together construct the phenomenal world. It has however lately been growing apparent that all attempts to conceive the unrepresented in terms of idol-matter in idol-space and idol-time break down. Approaching it this way, we learn only that by taking it up into mathematical equations we can produce startling technological results.

Two consequences seem to follow. Firstly, it would be rash to assume that there is no other approach than the mathematical one. Who can affirm, and on what evidence, that we may not also learn to approach the unrepresented by way of enhancing our figuration,[1] so as to make it a conscious process, as well as by the path of mathematical hypothesis? For sensation and figuration are the—at present unconscious—moment in which we actually meet the unrepresented (or, at least, encounter its resistance) in experience, as distinct from applying alpha-thinking to it afterwards. In this way we should gradually eliminate the unrepresented by rendering it phenomenal. It, too, would take its place among the collective representations. We

---

[1] As Goethe did (cf. p. 138).

should then at least find out whether what I have said about the phenomena can, or cannot, in the last resort be applied to the (as yet) unrepresented also; that is to say, whether or no they are representations of the collective unconscious. Certainly, the 'something quite vague' which can be coaxed into producing an atomic explosion does not look much like a collective unconscious—but then neither did the *represented*, which underlies the ordinary appearances, look like one—until we started thinking seriously about them.

Secondly, it would be rash to dismiss out of hand that different, and essentially representational, conception of time and space, which I mentioned at the beginning of this chapter. Which of the two is the *cul de sac* and which is the highway; whether it is more practical and straightforward, and whether the human mind is likelier to get somewhere, by thinking of man as surrounded by a cosmos or sphere of wisdom; or by thinking that space is spherical and the universe of finite size, although unbounded and getting bigger, are questions which everyone will decide for himself. It is, at all events, the former conception (as the reader will by now be aware) upon which the whole argument of this book converges; and from now on I shall assume its validity.

We may think of the cosmic wisdom as related to the appearances rather as, in men, the inner, unspoken word (the *verbum cordis, verbum intellectus*, of which Aquinas wrote) is related to the word (*vox*) that is actually vocalized. At least it is only on some such basis that we can ever hope to understand such a phenomenon as the history and literature of the Jews, or its culmination in Christianity, in a way which does not simply cut us off from the accumulated wisdom and insight of the past.

In Chapter XVI something was said of the part played by the Jewish impulse in the development of the Western world. If we would go farther and consider its place in the whole history of man, we can, I believe, best do so by reflecting on the nature of *memory*. Just as, when a word is formed or spoken, the original unity of the 'inner' word is polarized into a duality of outer and inner, that is, of sound and meaning; so, when man himself was 'uttered', that is, created, the cosmic wisdom became polarized, in and through him, into the duality of appearance and intelligence, representation and consciousness. But when creation has become polarized into consciousness on the one side and phenomena, or appearances, on the other, memory is made possible, and begins to play an all-important part in the process of evolution. For by means of his memory man makes the outward appearances an inward experience. He acquires his self-consciousness from them. When I experience the phenomena in memory, I make them 'mine', not now by virtue of any original participation, but by my own inner activity. It is from this activity in memory, it will be recalled, that the human word, according to Aquinas, 'proceeds'. For, once the phenomena are 'mine', I can reproduce them in the form of words.

Thus, the human word, for Aquinas (as we saw in Chapter XIII), proceeds from the memory, as the Divine Word proceeds from God the Father. We shall understand the place of the Jews in the history of the earth, that is, of man as a whole, when we see the Children of Israel occupying the position in that history which memory occupies in the composition of an individual man. The Jews, with their language trailing vestiges of the world's Creator and their special awareness of history, were the dawning memory in the human race. They too tore the phenomena from their setting of original participation and made them inward, with intent to reutter them from within as word. They cultivated the *inwardness* of the represented. They pinpointed participation to the Divine Name, the I AM spoken only from within, and it was the logic of their whole development that the cosmos of wisdom should henceforth have its perennial source, not without, and behind the appearances, but within the consciousness of man; not in front of his senses and his figuration, but behind them.

# XXIII

## RELIGION

When one ventures to speak, as I did in Chapter XIX, of man standing 'in a directionally creator relation' to the phenomena, it is clear that a theological issue is raised. Religion is essentially an 'I-Thou' relation between man on the one hand and the Creator of man and of his phenomena, on the other. A man who cannot think of his Creator as a Being other than himself cannot be said to have a religion. This is a truth of which modern theology, in its reaction against the vague creative-evolutionism, which sometimes passed muster as religion in the nineteenth century, is very much and very healthily aware.

Unfortunately, it is just on the interpretation and application of this all-important truth that our modern idolatry has fastened its claws. For idolatry has coarsened the very meaning of 'otherness'—the very way in which 'other' and 'same' can be thought. We have seen, in Chapter XIII, how distinctions not determined by the senses were once concrete experiences, before they faded away into the 'frigidity' of subjective ideas with the coming of the scientific revolution. We have seen, for instance, how Schiller was unable to conceive that Goethe's *Urphänomen* could be anything at all, unless it was *either* a phenomenon perceivable by the passive senses, *or* an abstract idea. So to the typical modern mind, fixed firm in its idolatry, unless God is thought of as not merely other than itself, but other *in the phenomenal mode* and after the manner in which the idols are other, God must be merely an idea.

Yet this can be no more than a passing blindness. Once it was remembered, and some day it will be realized afresh, that 'the soul is in a manner all things', God the Father is not less, but *more* 'other' from me than are the phenomena. But, if I think of Him as other *in the same mode* as the phenomena, then I substitute an idol for Him; and if I then proceed to worship Him so thought of, then, whatever I may *say* about it, in the secret recesses of my soul I am worshipping—perhaps some kind of guardian angel, certainly not my Creator. In order to be sure of distinguishing him numerically from myself, and in the name of humility, I have dared to think of him as an existence *parallel* with my own. Herein lies the idolatry which infects contemporary religion.

We saw, in Chapter XVI, how the willed ousting of participation, which was the paramount impulse, or obedience, of the Jews, could contribute to the same result as did the alpha-thinking of the Greeks and their successors. But we saw also how a waxing experience of the *inwardness* of the Divine Name was the proper counter-pole to their loss of original participation. We stopped short, however, of the point where this experience was lost. By the time Jesus was born the Divine Name had ceased to be spoken by man in the Temple or elsewhere. The pharisees had made it the name of a Being exclusively objective, remote, inaccessible, infinitely superior to, yet imagined as existentially parallel with man. Thus, the Jews had barely glimpsed, before they again lost sight of, that which is the opposite pole to man's otherness from the I AM, namely his supreme identity with it.

The fixing of such a gulf between God and man was not fatal to religion so long as some measure of original participation remained. To a participating consciousness, apprehending the world and the word as image, many nouns are the names of the Creator ('non proprie sed per similitudinem') and the noun *God* is merely one of them. To a nonparticipating consciousness, apprehending the world as object, most nouns are the names of idols and the noun *God* can be no exception.[1]) If the noun *God* were indeed the Divine Name, it would not frequently appear in discourse as the subject of easy and familiar sentences. Whereas, in fact, it is long now since this liberty became almost the recognized mark by which we distinguish the sermon from other forms of utterance. The progressive loss of original participation necessarily involves one of two alternatives, *either* an ever-increasing experience of the inwardness of the Divine Name and the Divine Presence—which is the religious aspect of what I have called 'final participation'—*or* an ever-increasing idolatry, in religion as elsewhere.

This dilemma I believe to be the ultimate and innermost significance of Protestantism, the development of which has been roughly contemporary with that of the scientific revolution. For the idolatry of which I have just written is, of course, not the whole story. In many corners, in many movements, both within and without the established churches, a new impulse towards final participation has gathered strength, as men have attempted to make the Pauline maxim: 'Not I, but Christ in me' a living experience. 'Though God be everywhere present,' wrote William Law (author of the 'Serious Call'):

> yet He is only present to thee in the deepest and most central part of thy soul. Thy natural senses cannot possess God, or unite thee to Him; nay, thy inward faculties of Understanding, Will and Memory can only reach after God, but cannot be the place of His habitation in thee. But there is a root or depth in thee, from whence all these faculties come forth, as lines from a centre, or as branches from the body of the tree. This depth is called the Centre, the Fund or Bottom of the soul. This depth is the Unity, the Eternity, I had almost said the Infinity of thy soul; for it is so infinite that nothing can satisfy it, or give it any rest but the infinity of God.[2]

[1] Cf. Aquinas. *Summa* Ia, qu. 13, a 9.
[2] *The Spirit of Prayer*, Part I, ch. 2.

This, on the one side, and on the other that valiant attempt, which began with the Reformation and ended in Fundamentalism, to understand and accept literally—*and only literally*—the words of the Bible, precisely while their meanings were being subtly drained away by idolatry—these are the opposite and complementary poles between which Protestantism has hitherto revolved.

If this book has succeeded in showing anything, it has shown that the only possible answer to the idolatry with which all our thinking is to-day infected, is the acceptance and conscious ensuing of that directionally creator relation to the phenomenal world, which we know to be a fact, whether we like it or not. Is God's creation less awe-inspiring because I know that the light, for instance, out of which its visual substance is woven, streams forth from my own eyes? 'Look upon the rainbow,' wrote the author of *Ecclesiasticus*:

> Look upon the rainbow, and praise him that made it:
> very beautiful it is in the brightness thereof.
> It compasseth the heavens about with a glorious circle,
> and the hands of the most High have bended it.

Do I echo these words less warmly, when I recollect that יהוה is creating the rainbow through my eyes? When I know that to think otherwise is an illusion or a pretence? Does piety depend on original participation? If so, one thing is certain; there is no future for it. But fortunately it does not. I did not create my eyes. And if an understanding of the manner of my participation in the appearance of a rainbow does not diminish my awe before its Creator, why should that be the case with the other more palpable phenomena? What but idolatry could ever make me suppose it *was* the case? 'Let not your heart be troubled: ye believe in God, believe also in me.'

I did not create my eyes. But we saw at the beginning of this book how, in order that the world of appearances may arise, it is not enough for the senses alone to be added to the unrepresented. That world depends no less on man's figuration; and, with that, also on his imagination. It is because imagination participates the creative activity in this way that it has itself been dimly felt to be, and described as, 'creative'. We saw in Chapter XXI how this means that the future of the phenomenal world can no longer be regarded as entirely independent of man's volition. This is the difference between original and final participation.

This is also a conclusion from which piety may shrink. We must then ask ourselves (apart altogether from our obligation to accept the truth because it is true) whether we *ought* to shrink from the notion that we are to share the responsibility of maintaining an earth which it has already, it seems, been given into our hands to destroy. Moreover, has history any real significance unless, in the course of it, the relation between creature and Creator is being changed?

> God's view is the view of mind as such, for it corresponds to the real structure of existence. The tendency of any mind, in proportion as it overcomes its creaturely limitations, must be to gravitate towards the divine centre, and share the divine view of things. That is the goal; it cannot be the starting-point.[1]

Has history any significance, unless we can apply these words to the whole development of the mind of man? Would it not be wiser, instead of shrinking, to recall the words of St. Paul: *For the earnest expectation of the creature waiteth for the manifestation of the sons of God*—and the German poet, Novalis's gloss: *Man is the Messiah of nature?*

On the other hand, it may be objected that all this talk of the relation of man to the phenomenal world is cold stuff, having little or nothing to do with religion, whose field is the soul and its salvation. But this 'watertight' attitude is itself a product of idolatry. What the Psalmist wrote of the old idols is true no less of the idols of the twentieth century.

[1] Austin Farrar, *A Rebirth of Images*. Dacre Press. 1949.

'They that make them are like unto them.' The soul is in a manner all things, and the idols we create are built into the souls of our children; who learn more and more to think of themselves as objects among objects; who grow hollower and hollower. In the long run we shall not be able to save souls without saving the appearances, and it is an error fraught with the most terrible consequences to imagine that we shall.

Let us not, nevertheless, be unduly oppressed by the fear of losing all we are accustomed to, whether it be that delight in a wholly independent world of nature of which I spoke in Chapter XXI, or of some special brand of piety that depends on it. But let us make no mistake as to the magnitude of the moral demand which is made on us. In that respect there is no need for the moralist to worry. It is not such cold stuff after all. The world of final participation will one day sparkle in the light of the eye as it never yet sparkled early one morning in the original light of the sun. But the coming of this light presupposes a goodness of heart and a steady furnace in the will, which have only not been emphasized in this book, because they are not the subject of it.

The morality of imagination is subtle and deep and far-reaching—subtle above all, because imagination itself is still in its tender infancy. I have already pointed out that imagination and goodness are *not* synonymous. But I believe that, if we are sensitive to it, we may divine in this age a very close and special relation between them. This relation was the guiding intuition of that great, confused spirit—the very St. George of iconoclasm—William Blake, who held that Imagination is the cardinal virtue, because the literalness which supports idolatry is the besetting sin, of the age which is upon us. But we must walk warily here.

It is in the nature of the case that, if at any point in time something like a *new* moral demand is made on humanity, moral judgments grow for a time double and confused. Thus, in Chapter XIX I spoke of certain 'symptoms of iconoclasm', in the shape of a new willingness to apprehend symbolically. If I now maintain that these have a moral significance, and indeed a paramount moral significance, I am at once in the difficulty that the scale of values I have set up not only does not correspond with the generally accepted scale of Christian moral values, but appears to cut right across it. There are plenty of people with a natural taste for dream-psychology, or for art or literature of a symbolical nature, for sacramentalism in religion, or for other things whose meaning cannot be grasped without a movement of the imagination, who are arrogant or self-centred or in other ways no better than they should be. And conversely there are prosaic, humdrum, literal souls before whose courage and goodness we are abashed. It is not a happy task to have to maintain that, from one point of view, and that an all-important one, the former must be accounted morally superior. But then neither would it have been a happy task to have to maintain, let us say, to a disciple of Rabbi Hillel, that from one point of view and that an all-important one, some of the more raffish members of St. Paul's congregation at Corinth possessed the one thing needful which the Rabbi lacked. The 'needful' virtue is that which combats the besetting sin. And the besetting sin to-day is the sin of literalness,[1] or idolatry. Relative moral values are not as simple as relative places in class at school. There is a tragedy of progress.

And yet in neither case, perhaps, to a fine and sincere moral intuition, is the apparent irrelevance as total as I have just suggested. The relation between the mind and heart of man is a delicate mystery, and hardness is catching. It will, I believe, be found that there *is* a valid connection, at some level however deep, between what I have called 'literalness'

[1] It is at this point that I can most happily acknowledge the very real debt which my book owes to stimulus and enlightenment derived from the conversation and writings of my friend Mr. Roger Home. Indeed the recollection of his *saeva indignatio* on the subject of 'literalness' may well have been the catalyst, without which a rather wayward collection of notes and ideas would never have taken shape as a book at all.

and a certain hardness of heart. Listen attentively to the response of a dull or literal mind to what insistently presents itself as allegory or symbol, and you may detect a certain irritation, a faint, incipient aggressiveness in its refusal. Here I think is a deep-down moral gesture. You may, for instance, hear the literal man object suspiciously that he is being 'got at'. And this is quite correct. He is. Just as he is being 'got at' by his unconscious through the symbolism of his dreams. An attempt is being made, of which he is dimly aware, to undermine his idols, and his feet are being invited on to the beginning of the long road, which in the end must lead him to self-knowledge, with all the unacceptable humiliations which that involves. Instinctively he does not like it. He prefers to remain 'literal'. But of course he hardly knows that he prefers it, since self-knowledge is the very thing which he is avoiding.

We could pursue the matter further and instance, on the positive side, a certain humble, tender *receptiveness* of heart which is nourished by a deep and deepening imagination and by the self-knowledge which that inevitably involves. Perhaps this is what Blake had in mind, when he called Imagination 'the Divine Body of the Lord Jesus, blessed for ever'; but we have digressed too far already from the main road.

One final word, however, before we leave the specifically moral aspect behind us. It may be objected that however true it may be, all that I have been saying is much too difficult to have much to do with the religion of ordinary men. This is not an objection which would have appealed to St. Augustine or the Fathers of the Church, but let us consider it. In the first place, a great deal of the complexity of my argument is due to the deep-seated error, with its consequently innumerable ramifications, which that argument has sought to unravel. The movements of fingers disentangling a crumpled skein are complicated, but the final result is not complication. Secondly, from one point of view God is always simple, as the light is simple, and the simplest soul can turn to Him at whatever point it stands in the matter of education or wisdom. But from another, since He is everywhere present, He must be at least as complicated as the most complicated thing in His creation. God's view is 'the view of mind as such'—and outside idolatry we cannot really separate His 'view' of creation from creation itself —except as the Persons of the Trinity are 'separate'.

There is, moreover, a topical application of this truth. In the industrial and urbanized civilization of to-day many of the 'simple' minds which meet with indifference or with indignant protest any suggestion of difficulty or complexity in theology, are not so simple when it comes to tackling the complexities of the phenomenal world in nature or machinery. The relation between the mind and heart of man is indeed a close and delicate one and any substantial cleft between the two is unhealthy and cannot long endure. Hence, however the case may stand for the time being, or with a few individuals here and there, it is certain that the mind of man as a whole cannot safely be left to occupy itself with idols, while a moral, or even an adoring 'ghost in the machine' responds to the otherness of God with love and obedience and the cultivation of self-improvement.

There will be a revival of Christianity when it becomes impossible to write a popular manual of science without referring to the incarnation of the Word. It is these books, not popular theology (however excellently and simply it is written, as to-day it often is) on which the mind of the proletariat seizes as it awakens from its ancient peasant-dreaming and peasant-wisdom. It is these—especially if they are laced with Marxism—which the needy oriental student in Bloomsbury devours and takes home with him; it is these which up to now are the answering legacy of the West to the East, whence she once derived her religion. The hungry sheep look up and are not fed. But Marxism forges ahead, because the scientific outlook (which is in the blood of the proletariat, because it is in the collective representations to which they are awakening) is part and parcel of its message;

whereas to Christian doctrine, as now presented, it is at worst a stumbling-block and, at best, totally irrelevant.

I have tried to show in this book that it is in fact very far from irrelevant; inasmuch as the scientific revolution marked a crucial stage in that evolution from original to final participation, which is the progressive incarnation of the Word. I have tried to show that the phenomena cannot be understood in their true nature without an understanding of precisely that evolution.

In a letter to *The Times* last year, concerning the evangelical mission of Dr. Graham, the Bishop of Plymouth wrote:

> . . . Our Lord constantly emphasized his healing ministry to the whole man; if he is not Lord of our minds, he is not the saviour whom this generation, which is our immediate concern, so sorely needs.

I am persuaded that in our time the battle between the powers of good and evil is pitched in man's mind even more than in his heart, since it is known that the latter will ultimately follow the former. In the Christian doctrine of the Trinity the Logos, or Word, is one of the three Persons. The conception of a threefold nature in the Godhead is not, however, peculiar to Christianity. It is to be found also in oriental religions and is perhaps the formal principle underlying the whole complicated organism of Greek mythology. It is the *depth* of all theology. What is peculiar to Christianity is the nexus which that acknowledges between the Second Person of the Trinity and a certain historical *event in time*. For the Christian, accordingly, religion can never be simply the direct relation between his individual soul and the eternal Trinity. As long as we ourselves are occupying a standpoint in time, so long, interposed between the First and Third Persons, all history, in a manner, lies.

Not to realize to the uttermost the otherness of God from ourselves is to deny the Father. But equally, not to strive to realize the sameness—to renege from the Supreme

Identity—is to deny the Holy Spirit. This, any deeply religious man may feel, whatever terminology he may have
learnt to employ. To this a true Christian—or so it seems to
me—must add: In no way to relate the former with the past,
and the latter with the future of the world, is to seek to
deprive history, and perhaps time itself, of all religious
significance.

# XXIV

# THE INCARNATION OF THE WORD

When we look back on past periods of history, we are often confronted with inconsistencies and blind spots in human thinking, which to us are so palpable that we are almost astonished out of belief. We find it hard to credit the inescapable fact that they remained, for decades or for centuries, completely invisible not only to the generality of men but also to the choicest and wisest spirits of the age. Such are the Athenian emphasis on liberty—with the system of slavery accepted as a matter of course; the notion that the truth could be ascertained and justice done with the help of trial by battle; the Calvinist doctrine of pre-election to eternal damnation; the co-existence of a Christian ethic with an economic doctrine of ruthless *laissez-faire*; and no doubt there are other and better examples.

I believe that the blind-spot which posterity will find most startling in the last hundred years or so of Western civilization, is, that it had, on the one hand, a religion which differed from all others in its acceptance of time, and of a particular point in time, as a cardinal element in its faith; that it had, on the other hand, a picture in its mind of the history of the earth and man as an evolutionary process; and that it neither saw nor supposed any connection whatever between the two.

I have offered my own explanation of this curiosity by pointing, as I did in Chapter IX, to the heavy weight of idolatry which rested on the Western mind at the time when the theory of evolution first appeared. To this must be added the marked reluctance of Christians to admit any sort of relation between their own religion and any religion which preceded it, except the Jewish, and latterly not much even with that. St. Augustine, it is true, affirmed that there had always been one true religion and that after the Incarnation this was called Christianity.[1] But the general tendency has been all the other way; and the study of comparative religions, which is still hardly a hundred years old, met at first, if any attempt was made to apply it to Christianity, with the same implacable hostility, though it now shows some signs of relenting. The loss of any participating experience of time may, I have suggested elsewhere, have something to do with this. To idolatry an event is *either* historical *or* symbolical. It cannot be both. There was accordingly a great, and in the circumstances a not wholly unjustified, fear. If it were once admitted that, for example, the Corn-god or the mystery religions had any significance for Christianity, or led up to it in any way, Christianity would itself promptly be assumed to be 'derived from' these religions and would dissolve away into anthropology and symbolism.

Whatever the explanation, the fact is very strange. When the horizon of time expanded suddenly in the nineteenth century, one would have expected those who accepted evolution and remained Christians, to see the incarnation of their Saviour as the culminating point of the history of the earth—a turning-point of time to which all at first led down and from which all thereafter was to lead upward. Moreover, having regard to the antiquity now attributed to the earth and man, one would have expected them to feel that we are still very very near to that turning-point, indeed hardly past it; that we hardly know as yet what the Incarnation means; for what is two thousand years in comparison with the ages which preceded it?

This is not in fact what is thought and felt by the relatively

[1] *Retractationes*, I, xiii, 3.

small number of people who still believe in the Incarnation. I have found that, when they are pressed to 'make sense', as it were, of the ages which preceded the birth of Christ—in which men also lived and died—the practice is to achieve it by postulating a retrospective effect of the Incarnation. This is indeed to abandon an idol-notion and to accept a participating or imaginal notion of time. But surely it also involves a sudden and uneasy jump in thought from time to eternity![1] Such a leap cuts itself off, by refraining, from an understanding of the phenomenal world and is thus more appropriate to oriental and pre-Christian religion than to the time-embracing religion of the West.

Look here upon this picture and on this! The stumbling-blocks will only disappear when we substitute for the false picture, in our minds, of an evolution of idols, that other true picture of the evolution of phenomena. We have seen how original participation, which began as the unconscious identity of man with his Creator, shrank, as his self-consciousness increased, and how this was associated with the origin and development of language. We have seen how, in the last few centuries B.C. it had contracted to a faint awareness of creative activity alike in nature and in man, to which was given the name of the Logos or Word. And then, we have seen (in Chapter XIX) the first faint premonitory symptoms of final participation appearing already in the first centuries of our era.

Between these two phases—if we meditated deeply enough on the nature and development of meaning in language—we could, if necessary, infer without other help, that the turning-point of time must have occurred. We could infer that the incarnation of the Word must have culminated.

What in fact happened according to the record? In the heart of that nation, whose whole impulse it had been to eliminate original participation, a man was born who

[1] Deeply as I admire it, this would be my criticism of the theology of the late Charles Williams.

simultaneously identified himself with, and carefully distinguished himself from, the Creator of the world—whom he called the Father. On the one hand: 'I am not alone, but I and the Father that sent me,' etc. On the other: 'I and the Father are one,' etc. In one man the inwardness of the Divine Name had been fully realized; the final participation, whereby man's Creator speaks from within man himself, had been accomplished. The Word had been made flesh.

In other men—though we have pointed to certain (mainly trivial) premonitory symptoms—that conscious realization has still barely begun to show itself. Except that the tender shoot of final participation has from the first been acknowledged and protected by the Church in the institution of the Eucharist. For all who partake of the Eucharist first acknowledge that the man who was born in Bethlehem was 'of one substance with the Father by whom all things were made'; and then they take that substance into themselves, together with its representations named bread and wine. That is after all the heart of the matter. There was no difficulty in understanding it, as long as enough of the old participating consciousness survived. It was only as this faded, it was only as a 'substance' behind the appearances gradually ceased to be an experience and dimmed to a hypothesis or a credo, that the difficulties and doctrinal disputes concerning trans-substantiation began to grow.

But, by the physical act of communion as such, men can only take the Divine substance, the 'Name apart' directly into the unconscious part of themselves; by way of their blood. And in this, as we saw in Chapter XII, we participate in two ways—both outwardly as a mere appearance (and, at present, therefore an idol) and inwardly by original participation. Thus, the relation between original and final participation in the Eucharistic act is, as we should expect, in the utmost degree complex and mysterious. If we accept at all the claims made by Christ Jesus concerning his own mission, we must accept that he came to make possible in the course of time the transition of all men from original to final participation; and we shall regard the institution of the Eucharist as a preparation—a preparation (we shall not forget) which has so far only been operant for the sidereally paltry period of nineteen hundred years or so.

To speculate, in a theological or cosmological context, on what might have been if things had gone otherwise, is from one point of view absurd. It is certainly foolish, if not blasphemous, to do so for the sake of doing so. But as a *means* to a better understanding of what has been and is, such speculation may be illuminating. The whole depth and poignacy of Augustine's *felix peccatum Adae!*[1] would be lost on anyone who was not prepared to suppose, even for an instant, that Adam might not have fallen.

With this end in view, then, we may permit ourselves to ask what would have happened if the incarnation of the Word had been understood at the time when it occurred; if Christ had been acknowledged instead of being crucified. In fact, by the time the Event happened, the pharisaical element in Jewish religion had apparently triumphed, balking the nation of the opportunity of fulfilling its destiny. Instead of realizing the inwardness of the Divine Name—a consummation to which their whole history had been leading—the Children of Israel had turned aside. The Name had ceased to be uttered even by the priests in the temple, and the Creator had been removed to an infinite external distance, as a Being, omnipotent indeed, and infinitely superior, but, in the way He was thought of, existentially parallel with man himself.

Yet—so we may speculate—this *need* not have happened. On the contrary, precisely the pharisees should hardly have needed even reminding of their nation's destiny by the Saviour's pregnant words; they should have leaped instantly into recognition of man's Creator speaking with the voice and through the throat of a man. Logically there was the possibility of a gentle, untragic transition from original

[1] 'Fortunate sin of Adam!'

to final participation, the one maturing in proportion as the other faded. Within the limits of this sort of speculation we can even say that it was this which was 'intended'. For the whole tenor of the Old Testament suggests that the imaginal consciousness characteristic of original participation was being destroyed, precisely in order that it might be reborn, 'The rejection of idolatry', writes Dr. Austin Farrar,[1]

> meant not the destruction but the liberation of the images. Nowhere are the images in more vigour than in the Old Testament, where they speak of God, but are not he . . . there is no historical study more significant than the study of their transformation. Such a transformation finds expression in the birth of Christianity; it is a visible rebirth of images.

That rebirth, however, did not take place. The crucifixion did.

Original participation fires the heart from a source outside itself; the images enliven the heart. But in final participation —since the death and resurrection—the heart is fired from within by the Christ; and it is for the heart to enliven the images.

Once again, later—once perhaps, towards the close of the Graeco-Roman, Aristotelian age—we can speculate on a similar possibility which was never realized. Once more, we are made to feel, 'there was a chance' that the requisite transition should be accomplished with relative smoothness and without the loss being first experienced to the full. For by that time there had appeared many Christened minds, which were capable of holding together, as it were in tension, the non-representational religious consciousness characteristic of the Jews and the representational consciousness derived from Greece and Rome. Dionysius the Areopagite taught that God was at once 'anonymous' and 'polyonomous'—nameless and many-named. And his treatise on the *Divine Names*, to which I have already referred,

[1] *A Rebirth of Images.*

took deep hold of medieval thought. Aquinas's philosophy, and in particular perhaps the two kinds of participation which we find referred to in it (see Chapter XIII), seemed on the threshold of effecting the transition gently. For, while his participation by composition (subject and predicate, form and matter) is specifically Aristotelian and looks backward to original participation, his hierarchical participation *per similitudinem*, derived in part from Dionysius, looks rather forward to the 'final' variety. And already, before Aquinas's time, the startlingly sudden rise and spread throughout Europe of a rich crop of legends of the Holy Grail suggests an attempted uprush of the Eucharistic mystery from a substantially unconscious to a substantially conscious—and extra-sacerdotal—status.

To do more than mention such things here would be to go too far. It is enough that the possibility, if such it was, was not realized. Instead, before final participation could be said to have well begun, the collective representations, 'the images', were swept clean of the last vestige of original participation by that intellectual pharisaism, begotten (but again not *necessarily* so) of the scientific revolution.

It is time to return from the abstractions of what might have been to the concrete reality of what has been and is.

# XXV

# THE MYSTERY OF THE KINGDOM

It was pointed out in Chapter XXIII that the attainment
by humanity of a new moral standpoint may mean doing
violence to moral judgments. Some violence is inevitable
when men are called on, in any sphere, not to *correct* their
previous ideas by removing some error, but actually to
move forward to a new plane that includes, rather than
replaces, the old. In the moral sphere, what was until now
simply 'good', is seen for the first time no longer as an
absolute, but also as the enemy of a better—and yet it has
still also to be grasped as good. This 'tragedy of progress',
as I called it, is the source of most of the 'hard sayings' in the
Gospels. Consider for instance the parables of the labourers
in the vineyard, and of the prodigal son. Our deep-rooted
feeling for the goodness of justice and equity has to be
outraged, because we are being beckoned towards a position
directionally opposite to the usual one; because we are
invited to see the earth, for a moment at all events, rather as
it must look from the sun; to experience the world of man
as the object of a huge, positive outpouring of love, in the
flood of whose radiance such trifles as merit and recompense
are mere irrelevancies.

Now there are no harder sayings to be found in The
Gospels than the group which deal with the use and purpose
of parabolic utterance. Take for instance the verses which
follow immediately after the parable of the sower in the
13th Chapter of St. Matthew (vv, 9–13):

Who hath ears to hear, let him hear.

And the disciples came, and said unto him, Why speakest thou unto them in parables?

He answered and said unto them, Because it is given unto you to know the mysteries of the Kingdom of Heaven, but to them it is not given.

For whosoever hath, to him shall be given, and he shall have more abundance; but whosoever hath not, from him shall be taken away, even that he hath.

Therefore speak I to them in parables: because they seeing, see not; and hearing, they hear not, neither do they understand.

Pausing there for a moment, it must be admitted that if we try to accept all this just as it stands,[1] and without any context or key to its meaning, then, to say that it 'does violence' to moral judgments is an understatement. The surface-meaning is not just severe, it is brutal. Nor is there any substantial difference in that respect between the passage quoted and the parallel passages in St. Mark iv, 9–12 and St. Luke viii, 9–10. If we want to understand what was really in the mind of the Speaker, we have to go deeper. And first of all, we notice how it all leads up to a phrase which contains a marked echo of certain passages in the Old Testament:

Because they seeing, see not; and hearing, they hear not, neither do they understand.

Such echoes are frequent in the reported sayings of Jesus and

---

[1] I take the Gospels as they stand, treating them (whenever they may have been written) as valid records left by wise and deeply responsible men. A good many of the arguments which have been advanced in favour of dissecting them will, I believe, disappear with the idolatry (as I have here ventured to call it) which now obstructs our penetration of their deeper meaning. Meanwhile, those who may still prefer to follow Jülicher, C. H. Dodd, Jeremias and others, in writing off Matthew 9–13 and the parallels in Mark and Luke as later interpretations added by the primitive church, may also care to ponder whether the primitive church is likely to have understood rather more, or rather less, than the twentieth-century commentator of the actual content of this and other parables.

attention is often drawn to them in the margins of annotated Bibles. Clearly his whole diction was saturated with recollections of this nature, even when no precise allusion can be fixed. The New Testament is, in a sense, latent in the language of the Old. In this case, however, in St. Matthew's version of the discourse, the allusion to the Old Testament *is* both precise and explicit. For Our Lord continues immediately:

> And in them is fulfilled the prophecy of Esaias, which saith, By hearing ye shall hear, and shall not understand; and seeing ye shall see and shall not perceive;
>
> For this people's heart is waxed gross, and their ears are dull of hearing, and their eyes they have closed: lest at any time they should see with their eyes, and hear with their ears, and should understand with their heart and should be converted and I should heal them.

To trace the reverberation to its source, it is not enough simply to turn to the 6th Chapter of *Isaiah*. Eyes that see not, and ears that hear not—where have we met with them before? In those verses from the 115th Psalm which I have already quoted twice, in Chapters X and XVI. This Psalm was very familiar to Jewish ears. It is one of the six *Hallel* psalms, obligatory at many feasts, and according to the *Jewish Encyclopedia* would have been part of the 'hymn' that was sung by the Thirteen after the Last Supper. Moreover, they are repeated almost verbatim in the 135th Psalm:

> *The idols of the heathen are silver and gold, the work of men's hands.*
>
> *They have mouths, but they speak not: eyes have they, but they see not;*
>
> *They have ears, but they hear not: neither is there any breath in their mouths. They that make them are like unto them: so is every one that trusteth in them.*

Turn again to the book of *Isaiah* and read the 44th Chapter, which is concerned mainly with idolatry:

They that make a graven image are all of them vanity; and their delectable things shall not profit . . . he maketh a god, even his graven image: he falleth down unto it, and worshippeth it, and prayeth unto it, and saith, Deliver me; for thou art my god.

They have not known nor understood: for he hath shut their eyes that they cannot see; and their hearts that they cannot understand.

It will be clear that, in order to understand the enigmatic words which, in the Synoptic Gospels, are interposed between the parable of the Sower and its interpretation, we must hear sounding through them as an overtone both the voice of the prophet Isaiah and the familiar voice of the Psalmist inveighing against graven images. We cannot do otherwise than read them as alluding to idolatry.

But to what kind of idolatry? It is quite impossible to assume that the *primary* idolatry—that is, the worship of images as *numinous*—of which the Children of Israel had once been guilty, was in the mind of Jesus. For how is it possible to fit any such allusion into the context? Moreover that kind of idolatry was no longer a besetting sin; it was one that had practically ceased to exist among the Jewish people. Thus, Conder in his *Outlines of the Life of Christ*, emphasizing the moral degeneracy which prevailed among the Jews at the time of the Nativity, could write (my italics): '*Idolatry excepted*, the darkest pictures painted by the Old Testament prophets of ancient Israel were realized.'

Something has already been said in Chapter XVI of two different kinds of idolatry. It was not only the first and obvious kind of which the Old Testament prophets were aware. There are some twenty different Hebrew words which have been rendered 'idol' or 'image' in the Authorized Version, and in addition to the presence of a false or filthy spirituality, it is clear that the Hebrew writers associated with images the almost opposite notion of *emptiness* or *nothingness*—the absence of any spirituality whatsoever. It is also clear from the passages already quoted that it was this secondary view of idols which was conceived as likely to be transferred to the subjective state of the idolator:

> They that make them are like unto them; and so is every one that trusteth in them.

This subjective emptiness—which was perhaps also the 'wilderness' or 'lonely place' in which the Baptist is described as calling for 'repentance'—seems to be the psychic condition which is brought about when the elimination of participation has deprived the outer 'kingdom'—the outer world of images, whether artificial or natural—of all spiritual substance, while the new kingdom within has not yet begun to be realized. It is, as it were, the null point between original and final participation.

The particular parable which Jesus related in this way to idolatry was the parable of the Sower, but we are given to understand that what he said applied to all parables, and indeed that the ability to 'know' this parable was a sort of pre-condition for the understanding, or knowing, of any other.

> Know ye not this parable? And how then will ye know all parables?[1]

What is it then about this particular parable—of the Sower —which called for this particular comment? Let us listen, first of all, to the ringing cry with which the parable concludes:

> Who hath ears to hear, let him hear!

That is not peculiar to this passage. It is even a phrase which was used by other Rabbis as well as Jesus. But if we take the trouble to examine all the occasions on which he used the words, we shall find them always in association with the teaching of 'the Kingdom' within, of the light, be it of

---

[1] Mark iv, 13.

candle or of sun, that shines now from within, of movement
from within outward, as opposed to movement from without inward. And so here: the disciples are first told, 'Unto
you it is given to know the mysteries of the kingdom of
heaven,' or, according to St. Mark,[1] 'Unto you it is given
to know the mystery of the Kingdom of God; but for them
that are without all things happen[2] in parables.'

Then follows the interpretation, beginning with the one
brief, abrupt verse:

The sower soweth the word.

The parable, then, was about the sowing of the word, the
Logos, in earthly soil. It was an attempt to awaken his
hearers to the realization that this seed was within their own
hearts and minds, and no longer in nature or anywhere
without. We have seen something of the change in the
nature of all imagery and representation, which takes place
with the transition from original to final participation. But
'transition' is a misleading word for the violent change in
the whole *direction* of human consciousness which, in the
last resort, this must involve. Henceforth the life of the
image is to be drawn from within. The life of the image is
to be none other than the life of imagination. And it is of
the very nature of imagination that it cannot be *inculcated*.
There must be first of all the voluntary stirring from
within. It must be, not indeed self-created, but certainly
self-willed, or else—it is not imagination at all; and is therefore incapable of iconoclasm. Iconoclasm is made possible
by the seed of the Word stirring within us, as imagination.
From him that hath not this seed—of final participation—
there shall be taken away, even that residue—of original
participation—that he hath.

[1] Mark iv, 11.
[2] γίγνεται. A.V. and R.V. have: 'Unto them that are without all things
*are done* in parables.' It could also, conceivably, have been translated 'all things
are made in parables', on the analogy of the clause in the Nicene Creed referred
to on p. 170 ('by whom all things were made.'), where the same Greek verb is
employed.

# The Mystery of the Kingdom

Truly to grasp, or (if I may use the expression) 'twig' what is meant by the word and its sowing, involves some elementary grasp of, or feeling for, the nature of final participation, and therefore also of the nature of parabolic utterance. It is only possible to those in whom the word, however feebly, has already taken root. Conversely: to have no inkling whatever of what happens in the moment of parabolic utterance is to be incapable of grasping, or 'knowing', *any* parable, any metaphor, any symbol, any sacrament.

Therefore it is impossible that the main object which it is sought to achieve by parable should be helped by explanations. Only those in whom the seed has already sprouted, in whom the stirring has taken place, can benefit by any explanation. For them indeed it may help to turn the little they have into abundance. But for those who have as yet made no voluntary inward motion in the direction of iconoclasm, for those who have not suffered that change of direction of the whole current of a man's being—the *metanoia*, or turning about of the mind, for which the heart's name is 'repentance'—explanations are of no avail. They will merely substitute one sort of idol for another. The interpretation itself will still need interpreting, and that interpretation also they will inevitably misconstrue in terms of their idolatry. This is in fact what has happened to the tremendous rubric: 'The sower soweth the word.' And one can well imagine the reluctance with which Christ launched it on the ocean of idolatrous misunderstanding, where we still mostly find it to-day.

The sowing of the word is commonly assumed to be no more than a pictorial way of referring to preaching and missionary activity. But how can this possibly be so? If this simple parallel is *all* that was intended, why are we warned so solemnly that the power to grasp it pre-supposes access to 'the mystery of the kingdom'? Certainly the writer of St. Matthew's Gospel himself leaves us in no doubt of his convictions, namely, that both the springing to life in man of 'the Word of the Kingdom' and its embodiment in parable were something to which Jewish history had always been leading up. For later, in the same chapter, at the close of a series of parables and similes intended to suggest the Kingdom, he adds (alluding to the long, historical 78th Psalm):

> All these things spake Jesus unto the multitude in parables; and without a parable spake he not unto them;
>
> That it might be fulfilled which was spoken by the prophet saying, I will open my mouth in parables; I will utter things which have been kept secret from the foundation of the world.[1]

If on the other hand what is pointed to as the sowing of the word, is the coming of God himself into nature and man; if what is hidden in this and the other parables and mataphors concerning 'the kingdom' is the turning-point of time itself, is the change-over to that directionally creator relation which has already been referred to, then we should expect what we in fact find. We should expect these sayings to be the 'hardest' of all, and we should expect them to be connected with man's overcoming of idolatry through the help of an invented or man-made imagery; for that is the first, wavering step on the road that leads to final participation.

Nobody can truly 'receive' such sayings who is without some inkling of all that the word and the Incarnation of the Word stand for in human evolution. This I have tried to describe in this book in the fuller and more precise perspective in which it can be seen to-day; but an understanding of the essence of it, in a different, older perspective—that is, in Greek and Hebrew versions of a 'Logos' teaching—had already become possible, as we have seen, before Christ came to the earth. To this understanding he appealed in the hard sayings.

[1] Matthew xiii, 34 and 35.

Truly to imagine their effect on those of his followers who *had* the understanding, we must have ears to hear; to hear the Christ as the Representative of Humanity actually speaking to the handful in Palestine long ago. We shall recall, for instance, the great series of 'I am—' sayings in St. John's Gospel: 'I am the way, the truth, and the life. . . .' 'I am the light of the world. . . .' 'I and the Father are one . . .' and we shall reflect how near was the Aramaic dialect he spoke to Hebrew—so that at each 'I am' the disciples must almost have heard the Divine Name itself, man's Creator, speaking through the throat of man; till they can hardly have known whether he spoke to them or in them, whether it was his voice which they heard or their own.

Now the Jews, as we have seen, were not interested in phenomena. They were interested in morality. And in their civilization it was the world of morality, not the world of nature, which thinking of the alpha type had been engaged in converting from a fountain of life into a system of laws. Our own idolatry, our mental and sensuous pharisaism, had hardly yet arisen; it was the idolatry of moral pharisaism which had first to be broken. We need not be surprised that the other idolatry, always latent, is only becoming fully apparent in our own day. Final participation is indeed the mystery of the kingdom—of the kingdom that is to come on earth, as it is in heaven—and we are still only on the verge of its outer threshold. Two thousand years is a trifle of time compared with the ages which preceded the Incarnation. More than a thousand had to pass before the Western Church reached even that premonitory inkling of final participation which it expressed by adding the *Filioque* to the Creed, and acknowledging that the Holy Spirit proceeds from the Son as well as, originally, from the Father.

The elimination of original participation involves a contraction of human consciousness from periphery to centre (cf. Chapter XI)—a contraction from the cosmos of wisdom to something like a purely brain activity—but by the same token it involves an *awakening*. For we awake, out of universal—into self—consciousness. Now a process of awakening can be retrospectively surveyed by the sleeper only after his awakening is complete; for only then is he free enough of his dreams to look back on and interpret them. Thus, the possibility to look back over the history of the world and achieve a full, waking picture of his own gradual emergence from original participation, really only arose for man with the culmination of idolatry in the nineteenth century. He has not yet learned to make use of it.

As we do so, the story of that gradual emergence will lie outspread before us in a clearer and clearer light. And as the mystery of the kingdom more and more unfolds itself, the Church, nursing mother of the still barely nascent Christ-impulse in men, must inevitably be faced with grievous decisions. Nothing is easier than to criticize the Church out of a sort of smug enlightenment. But in truth the difficulty has been wellnigh insuperable of maintaining the indispensable firmness of continuity with past tradition, while at the same time the meanings of all her armoury of words were being quietly melted away from within by an idolatry which had grown up without reference to her. In the dry husks that remain problems and dilemmas have swollen and multiplied, which, as we have seen, simply did not exist for the old participating consciousness that gave birth to the liturgy and the creeds.

For instance, a non-participating consciousness cannot avoid distinguishing abruptly between the concept of 'man', or 'mankind', or 'men in general' on the one hand and that of 'a man'—an individual human spirit—on the other. This difficulty did not arise to anything like the same extent as long as original participation survived. Therefore our predecessors were able, quite inwardly, to accept the sin of Adam as being *their* original sin also. And therefore we are not—because, for us, Adam (if he existed) was after all—somebody else! This has brought with it the loss of the whole concept of the 'fallen' as an essential element in the make-up of human beings; which in its turn is responsible for the devastating shallowness of so much contemporary ethics and contemporary psychology.

With the doctrine of evolution the concept of 'man', as a thinkable entity, with a history behind him and a destiny in front of him, made a first confused reappearance. But, owing to the form which that doctrine took under the influence of the prevailing idolatry, this 'man' of evolution has no inner unity with the spirit of any particular individual man alive on earth at any particular moment. When the evolution of phenomena is substituted for our supposed evolution of idols,[1] it will, I believe, be seen without much difficulty that the evolution of the individual human spirit has always proceeded step by step with the evolution of nature; and that both are indeed 'fallen'. The biological evolution of the human race is, in fact, only one half of the story; the other has still to be told.

The awakened clarity of retrospect, to which I have recently referred, will, I am persuaded, be obliged to recognize that the gradual emergence of man from original participation amounts also to the gradual emergence of 'men' from 'man'; that it is not just the cumulative history of the race, but the biography, also, of each individual spirit. Nor do I see how this can fail to involve the recognition of individual prenatal existence—or rather existences. Some understanding of this seems to have been common to most men before the West emerged from the East, and began the systematic ousting of original participation, about three thousand years ago. A renewal of that lost insight will almost certainly be one of the first steps to be taken by religion through the rebirth in her of that cosmic wisdom, which is the source not only of the world of appearances, but also of man's changing relation to them.

I suspect that, for the Church, it will not be easy. It will not be easy for the nursing mother to accept the possibility that her charge has grown to need additional nourishment;

[1] Cf. Chapters ix and x.

or that revelation of the mystery of the kingdom was not turned off at the tap when the New Testament canon was closed, but is the work of an earth-time. Such a step will not be taken with ease; but in the end, if the Christ infuses my whole man, mind as well as heart, the cosmos of wisdom, with all its forgotten truths, will dwell in me whether I like it or not; for Christ *is* the cosmic wisdom on its way from original to final participation.

This book is a study in idolatry, and especially that last and greatest step in idolatry which we call the scientific revolution. In it I have drawn attention to the great benefits which this revolution has brought about. I could have said much more of this. Races which throughout the history of the world have never had enough to eat are being fed, while I write, by the great technocracy of America. I have alluded also to the priceless gifts of accuracy and precision. Yet, when the last balance comes to be struck between good and evil, I do not believe it will be these things for which men will remember the scientific revolution with thankfulness.

Man, said J. P. Sartre, is a being who is *condemned to freedom*. That is one way of looking at it. And it is the only way, if man himself is nothing but a hollow idol. But if man is not hollow, but is the theatre on which participation has died to rise again, then there is also another way of looking at it. If, in Christ, we participate finally the Spirit we once participated originally; if, in so doing, we participate one another—so that 'men' once more become also 'man'; if, in original participation, we were dreamers and unfree, and if Christ is a Being who can be participated only in vigilance and freedom, then what will chiefly be remembered about the scientific revolution will be the way in which it scoured the appearances clean of the last traces of spirit, freeing us *from* original, and *for* final, participation. And if what it produced thereby was, as I have suggested, a world of idols, yet, as Augustine of old could contemplate the greatest of evils and exclaim *Felix peccatum!* so we, looking steadily on that world, and accepting the burden of existential responsibility which final participation lays on us, may yet be moved to add:

*Felix eidolon!*

'Peor and Baalim Forsake their temples dim . . .' the other name for original participation, in all its long-hidden, in all its diluted forms, in science, in art and in religion, is, after all—paganism.

# INDEX

# Index

# Index

light, 19, 161, 163, 178
Linnaeus, 72, 116
literal, and literalness, 51, 53, 62, 73 f., 83, 87, 92, 135, 159, 161-3
logic (*see also* predication), 90, 98
logical positivism, 99n.
*logos*, 45, 128
Logos, the, 127, 167 f., 179, 181
Lorenz, 143

Machines, 51, 80, 143
macrocosm (*see* microcosm)
Maimonides, 114
'mana,' 32-3, 42, 111
Martianus Capella, 96
Marxism, 164
mathematics, 43, 46
matter, 16, 20, 173
'maya,' 148
meaning (*see also* language), 116 f., 142, 183
memory, 85, 126-7, 154-5
metaphor (*see also* parable, symbol), 73 f., 83, 118 f., 126, 181
microcosm and macrocosm, 77, 78 f., 103, 149
Mill, J. S., 69, 98
Milton, John, 48
mistakes, 27
models, 17, 38-9, 51, 54, 61-2, 135-6
morality, 160-3, 174, 184
Moses, 106, 109, 112 f.
movement, 69, 101 f., 148
Müller, Max, 42, 104, 118-20
myth and mythology, 42, 66, 110, 118, 125, 134, 164

Name, the Divine, 112 f., 132, 155, 157-8, 170
names (*see also* language, word), 84, 88, 90, 98, 105, 108
'Natura,' 86, 129

Neo-Platonism (*see also* Plotinus), 96, 129
New Testament, 174 f.
Newton, Isaac, 59, 101
Nominalism, 91
*nous* (*see also* intelligence), 45
Novalis, 160

Old Testament (*see also* Israel, Jews, Hebrew language), 112 f., 151, 172, 176-7

Pallas Athene, 109
pantheism, 130
parable, and parables (*see also* image, metaphor, symbol), 174 f.
participation, 12-13, 28 f., and throughout; (in Aquinas: 89 f.)
'participation mystique,' 31, 33-4
Paul, Saint, 158, 160, 162
perspective, 94, 149, 152
'phaenomena,' 47-8
phallic cults, 109
pharisees, 157, 171
Philo Judaeus, 125
Philostratus, 128
Phinehas, 109
physics, 11-13, 17, 23, 33, 38, 40, 43, 51, 54, 56, 59, 63-4, 65, 145, 153 and elsewhere
piety, 160-1, 164
planets, 45, 49, 68, 76-7
Plato, 44, 45, 54, 55, 62, 96 f., 107, 110, 148
Plotinus (*see also* Neo-Platonism) 84, 128
poetry, 75, 89, 127 f.
potential (and actual), 49, 85 f., 92-3, 100 f., 124, 136 f.
predication, 31, 90, 98-9, 173
prophecy, 151
Protestantism (*see* Reformation)

# *Index*